THOMAS ELMEZZI

THE MAN
WHO KEPT
THE SECRET

THOMAS ELMEZZI

THE MAN
WHO KEPT
THE SECRET

A BIOGRAPHY BY
ROBERT LOCKWOOD MILLS
WITH HARRY MAURER

Cover and Interior design by Thomas Morlock

JET Foundation Press
185 Great Neck Road – Suite 410
Great Neck, NY 11021

Manufactured in the United States of America

Cataloging in Publication Data
Mills, Robert Lockwood

Thomas Elmezzi
The Man Who Kept the Secret

ISBN: 0-615-12644-8

1. Biography

Library of Congress Control Number: 2004112444

This book tells a classic American success story. It is the story of a boy who grew up in a poor immigrant family in a poor neighborhood, and who, by means of brains, hard work, and old-fashioned values, rose to prominence in a mega-corporation and accumulated a sizable fortune—though not fame—along the way. If ever there was one, Thomas Elmezzi is an American boy who made good.

But this is more than a success story—or, better said, it is a story showing that there is more than one way to succeed. Tom Elmezzi, who recently turned 89, has not chosen to turn his success into the material trappings that usually accompany the achievement of wealth. He and his wife, Jeanne, have lived for 50 years in the same five-room rented apartment in Great Neck, New York. He has never owned a home, let alone vacation property, though he could comfortably afford both. He doesn't possess art treasures or a wine cellar. He was once part owner of a boat, but no more. His one self-indulgence is automotive: Tom drives a Cadillac Seville and recently bought a silver Rolls-Royce Corniche—an extravagance so unusual for Tom that it seems outlandish. Otherwise, Tom has conserved his fortune and is now devoting it to "helping people," he says, largely by creating and funding the JET Foundation, which will be aiding the needy and working for the betterment of mankind long after Tom passes away. Tom embodies an ideal central to most of the world's great religions:

to give is more rewarding than to receive. His life illustrates that generosity is the highest form of success.

⟨────◆────⟩

Tom Elmezzi is a small man—"even shorter now than I used to be," he observes—with a full head of white hair and eyes that radiate intense interest in the world from behind gold-rimmed glasses. His gait is sometimes unsteady now, his fingers twisted with arthritis. But he is still a dapper dresser in his light blue shirt, red knit vest and navy pin-striped trousers. His office at the Jet Foundation on Great Neck Road testifies to a lifetime of curiosity and travel. The shelves are crowded with books and magazines, ranging from *National Geographic* to *Gold Coins of the World*, from *The British Pharmacopoeia 1932* to the thriller *Dirty Work*. He collects scale models of famous buildings and monuments he has visited; among the dozens on display are the Vatican, St. Patrick's Cathedral in New York, the Supreme Court building, Notre Dame in Paris, and the Basilica in Mexico City. A vitrine houses a large collection of lead soldiers in old uniforms of various British regiments: the Ox & Bucks Light Infantry, the King's Own Scotch Borderers. It also shows off miniature train cars, enamel boxes, and a model Harley-Davidson motorcycle. Other shelves hold porcelain riders on Lipizzaner stallions, model fire engines, and a ceramic leopard, crouching and snarling.

Most of these objects were acquired during Tom's 43-year career at Pepsi-Cola and the company whose fate was intertwined with Pepsi in the 1930s, Loft's Candy. Tom played a central role in the growth of modern Pepsi from a brand name without a product to the giant it is today. "It's a $30 billion operation now," he marvels. "When I think of all the people who are associated with it all over the world, directly and indirectly, it's phenomenal. And I feel I'm still part of it, because I'm the only one alive from that time. They're all gone. That's one reason for me to write this book—I didn't want to do it in the first place, but some things have to be put straight."

Another thing he is especially eager to communicate is his deep gratitude to his native land. Tom was born just eight years after his father first traveled to America from Italy, and two years after his mother arrived. Yet like other self-made sons of immigrants, he feels a passionate appreciation for the United States and its history that outshines the patriotism of many Americans whose families have been here for hundreds of years. Much of this book will be told in Tom's own words, so we will let him speak for himself here: "I find that most people take our country for granted. I think the people of this country need to be more aware of what the Founding Fathers did in forming the United States of America. They were learned men, well-to-do men. And many of them lost everything. Some got killed. Some were hanged. Every American should remember what these fellows did, what they gave up for us to be allowed to live the way we're allowed to live, because no other country in the world has the same thing.

You can come into this country and do anything you want and go anywhere you want anytime you want. And it's not because we're all alike. In France, in Germany, in Italy, in England, most everyone is the same nationality, at least until recently. In this country, we're made up of people from all over. Yet you can come to this country and have all kinds of freedom.

"Why do I think people here don't appreciate what they have? Because they've never suffered. This country hasn't been invaded in a long time. Since the Civil War, there's been no devastation here, outside of Pearl Harbor and September 11. So people don't understand. Most Americans do not have and will never have the advantage I had, of going around different parts of the world and seeing the poverty, the prostitution, the slavery that still exists, and nobody is doing anything about it. Sure, people here worry about whether they can go to school, whether they'll have a job. But these are things you can accomplish yourself. You have to have a goal. I'll tell you a story: One time in 1957, we had a big snowstorm in New York. Big blizzard. It took me three hours to get from Great Neck to the 59th St. subway station, near the Pepsi building. I came up the steps of the subway and there was a blind girl coming up the steps, too. It had finished snowing, but it was two feet deep out there. Here was this girl, blind, with a cane. I said, 'Where are you going?' She said, 'To work.' I said, 'Where do you work?" She said, 'At the Lighthouse,' which was on 59th St. So I walked her to her door. I'll never forget that. Never. She was a small girl, coming up those steps, nobody else there to help her, but she was going to work. Pepsi had a building on Park

Avenue and a couple of annexes nearby, and we had maybe 2,000 people working there. Six of us showed up that day. A lot of them could have walked to the office easily. To think of this girl doing what she did drives me crazy. That's why I say people don't appreciate what they have.

"I have a goal. I call it Camelot, my quest for Camelot. I personally have not fulfilled my quest. I want to help people. I want to use my money to do the right thing, and I want people to help me without taking any personal interest in the money. I'm coming close but I haven't gotten there. That's my Camelot. It'll probably never happen. But I have to keep seeking it."

CHAPTER ONE

"My father," says Tom, beginning his story, "was of the old school. He never in any way abused any of us. All he had to do was look at us, and that was enough to get us to behave. He was the patriarch."

It's no surprise that Joseph Elmezzi was of the old school, for he came from the old country. On an unknown day in an unknown month in 1883, a tiny boy was left on the Wheel of Foundlings at the Santo Spirito Hospital in Rome, about two blocks from the Vatican. Pope Innocent III founded the hospital in the year 1200, and Pope Sixtus V expanded it in the late 15th Century. Today it covers several square blocks, serving the health needs of the poor. One of its extraordinary features is the Wheel of Foundlings (*Ruota degli Esposti*), which stands in the courtyard offering mothers of newborn babies a way to leave them for adoption with no questions asked. The wheel is a revolving carousel with a cage. The mother places her infant in the cage, turns the wheel, and hospital personnel on the other side receive the baby. These babies are identified as *Matris Ignotae* (mother unknown), wrapped in blue cloth, and a double cross sign is placed on their lower legs. They're fed, clothed, and raised by resident sisters, even given a rudimentary education if need be, until an adoption can be arranged. The process can take years, months, hours, or occasionally only minutes.

Giuseppe proved to be one of the lucky ones. On the very day he was left on the Wheel, a Signora Virgilio, from the nearby town of Salle, gave birth at the hospital. Her baby was stillborn. The nuns offered Sra. Virgilio the newest baby from the Wheel as a substitute—another little boy. She accepted. The process took minutes. The boy would grow up in Salle and be known as Giuseppe Elmezzi. Through his long life—Giuseppe died in 1967, one day short of his 84th birthday—he never learned the genesis of his surname. Had the biological father of Sra. Virgilio's stillborn child been a man named Elmezzi, to whom she wasn't married? Was Elmezzi Sra. Virgilio's maiden name? Giuseppe's children, two of whom survive, don't know. Both born in the United States, they never knew their grandmother, and no one else could say where the name Elmezzi came from.

Giuseppe Elmezzi actually emigrated twice, part of the great wave of Italian immigrants that flowed into the U.S. during the decades from 1870 to 1920. In 1906, at 22 or 23 years old, he sailed on the *Republic* and arrived at Ellis Island, where he was registered as Giuseppe. He soon anglicized his name to Joseph, as many immigrants did. He also soon returned to Salle and sailed again for America on board the *Moltke*, arriving on Oct. 11, 1909. His young wife, Maria, followed on the *Berlin* and disembarked on February 23, 1912. She brought with her 5-year-old Umberto, who later became "Robert," and 3-year-old Guido, who retained his Italian name.

Giuseppe's voyages followed a familiar pattern in that era—and indeed, in this one. Father came to America in search of work, usually any work he could get. He'd send money back right away, knowing that its purchasing power was far greater in the home country. Often, homesick, he would return to Italy after a few years, having made enough to make his family more comfortable. Others, if successful enough to afford the steamer fares, would send for Mother and the children. With hard work and a little luck, the family would become American citizens, as millions did.

Maria Battaglia Elmezzi, born in 1888, would bear five more children in America. Twin girls—or so the other kids were told—arrived near the end of 1912 and perished in the ravenous influenza epidemic of 1918-20, leaving behind no documentation of their brief lives, an information void that brought heartache to the survivors for decades. Research for this book, however, has unveiled a deception on the part of Joseph and Maria regarding the birth of these twins.

Thomas was born on Dec. 9, 1914, followed by two sisters: Angelina (married name Colangelo), who died in 1990, and Francesca (Gallo), who is Tom's one surviving sibling. Maria Elmezzi died in 1955, at age 67.

Tom and his siblings had always been told that twin sisters named Maria and Francesca had been born within a year of Maria's arrival in the United States, and that they had died at age 6 of flu. The Elmezzi children accepted this explanation, knowing that the post-World War I influenza epidemic had wiped out entire families. Later, however, they became suspicious of what they'd been told.

Their suspicions proved well founded.

According to New York City birth records for the Borough of Queens, Maria Elmezzi did give birth to twins on January 13, 1913, and one was a girl named Francesca. But the other was a boy, Rosario. And no death records exist for anyone named Elmezzi for any location in Queens during the years 1918-20.

It seems clear in hindsight that Joseph and Maria Elmezzi invented a story to disguise their giving up of Francesca and Rosario at birth, most likely for adoption through a church. Giving up babies was commonplace in that era, and churches often handled social matters that today fall to local governments. Regardless of how the babies' surrender was accomplished, the fact that the parents misrepresented the truth about one of the twins' gender suggests the influenza story was likewise a deception. If the twins had died at the age of 6, falsifying the gender of one would have been pointless.

But with both twins being girls, would it not have been less painful for Joseph, an Italo-American immigrant with a presumably patriarchal bias, to give them away? Is it not likely that "Rosario" was changed to "Maria" to make the surrender of the kids less psychologically difficult for a man who felt that male children were more to be cherished? Tom had long suspected that something was wrong with his parents' story about the twins, for if they had lived in the household until 1919, his oldest brother Robert, born in 1906, would have remembered them. So would Guido, three years Robert's junior. But neither did. For that reason, Tom urged the author of this book to look into the question. To this day, he wonders if he has a sister and/or brother still living, ignorant of their origins and perhaps even unaware of each other's existence. "Someplace out there," Tom muses, "I may have siblings. And I can't find them. I've tried everywhere. We were told they died during the Spanish influenza, but they didn't die. My parents gave them away because they couldn't afford them."

The Elmezzi family, like most immigrant families, was indeed poor. Joseph first found work as a laborer, "digging streets and sewers," says Tom. Later he got a job with the Consolidated Gas Works, still doing manual labor, and finally "he got a job with the city, paving streets. That's what he retired from. He had no education of any kind."

The Elmezzis settled in Astoria, Queens. Astoria is convenient to Manhattan on the B.M.T. subway line, and in the '10s and '20s it had the feel of a suburb. It was attractive to immigrants as an alternative to urban slum living, so it was largely a working-class neighborhood, with an enclave of mansions built by wealthy Manhattanites who summered along the East River. The Irish arrived first, escaping the potato famine of the late 1840s. When they first sought jobs in New York, they often found "No Irish Need Apply" signs posted by business owners, who were typically Protestant descendants of early Dutch and English settlers and saw the newcomers as rowdy drunkards. Their bias was as much anti-Catholic as anti-Irish. Against it the newcomers had little political ammunition, so they tended toward the trades, railroads, and docks, because someone was always needed to haul crates, hammer nails into ties, shovel coal and unload ships.

The Italian-Americans thus found themselves in the forefront of a nascent labor movement, one that gained momentum in the larger cities. Meanwhile immigrants to New York now included Italians, Germans, and Eastern Europeans, who became rivals for unskilled and semi-skilled jobs. Immigration and workers' issues were on a collision course as desperation for work met the fight for better conditions. Workers claimed an entitlement to higher wages, shorter hours, improved safety, and most controversially, the right to strike without being replaced. The last was considered anathema by the business owners, who viewed any striker as having quit voluntarily.

Enter newer immigrants like Giuseppe Elmezzi. Most had been poorly educated at home and faced language barriers, so they competed for whatever blue-collar jobs were available. Dock owners in particular found Italians generally indifferent to labor issues and willing to replace striking longshoremen. They'd work for a pittance, too. Naturally, management moved Italian immigrants into the jobs of Irish-born workers out on strike. This infuriated the strikers. It led to fights, labor unrest, and entrenched Irish-Italian enmity. In the case of the Elmezzis, this tension would play a key role in the family's choice of religion.

The Elmezzis moved several times within Astoria. Tom was born at 39 Willow Street on December 9, 1914. They later lived at 1 North William Street,

47 North William Street, and 10 LeBannon Terrace, before settling in for the final time, in 1928, at 1818 25th Road. Tom lived there from age 13 until he married at age 24. "It's a funny thing," he remembers. "In the house where I was born, we had plumbing. The next move, yes. The next move, no. Even the bathrooms were crude, nothing like what we have today. But in that third place, we had to go outside and walk about 30 feet to the outhouse. That was frightening for me, going out there at night. Then we went to another place, the house where I met my wife. The kitchen was on the first floor and had a kerosene stove. There was a hole in the ceiling so the heat could go up and heat the second floor.

"My father was a poor man, but he did the best he could in raising a family. We never were without what we needed. If we thought we weren't getting what we should, we'd make a little issue of it, and he would do it. One Christmastime, my older brother and I were sitting on the porch on Christmas day. He came home from work. If you're working for the gas works, someone has to run it on Christmas, and he was one of the laborers who had to go in on Christmas day. So he sees us and says, 'What's the matter?' My brother said, 'Well, we don't have any chicken.' My father never even came into the house. Turned around, went off, and somehow or other he got a chicken. Where he got it, I don't know, but it was a cleaned chicken.

"My mother was a dear woman, a dear woman. She struggled, and she did everything possible for us. She did a lot of our sewing and repairing. When I tell people we used to have undershirts made out of flour bags, they laugh at me. But that's what you had to do. And there was a Jewish man who used to come around selling cloth, so she'd buy whatever she needed and pay it off every week. I was 13 years old when I got my first suit. Father took me down to Delancey St., and for my birthday I got a suit. It cost thirteen dollars.

"We spoke mostly English in the home. My father spoke good English, and my mother finally spoke pretty good English too, but you could tell she had an accent. Whenever they went out with friends, they spoke Italian. I picked up a lot of Italian that way, but it wasn't spoken much in the home. We came to America, so we were Americans. My parents forgot about Italy. They never spoke about going back."

Joseph and Maria made another major change, too—in their religious affiliation. At some point before Tom was born—his father would never tell him the whole story—Joseph asked a priest in the local Catholic Church to help him with something. But the priests in Astoria were Irish-Americans for the most part. Many had been clerics in America for decades. Irish Catholics were generally faithful about attending mass, Italian-Americans less so; thus the hierarchy tended to see Italians as nominal Catholics who might keep sacramental tokens on their windowsills at home but wouldn't observe actual sacraments in church. And because of the labor conflicts and other cultural issues, there was little love lost between the two communities. So when Joseph, born and raised a Catholic in Italy, sought help from his neighborhood parish, he was turned down.

It's a measure of the man's reticence that he never confided in his children about what help he had needed. Had he been looking for a job reference? Was it financial assistance? Food? A babysitter? Given the recent discovery indicating that Joseph and Maria surrendered twin children in 1913, the best guess is that the couple felt they couldn't handle two babies at that point in their lives, asked the local priests to help arrange their relocation anonymously, and were told it wasn't possible. There was no Wheel of Foundlings in New York City.

But whatever the reason, Joseph never forgave the Catholic Church. He found the help he needed from an Italian pastor at the Astoria Italian Methodist Church, and from then on, that became the Elmezzis' place of worship. The church still stands, at 21st St. and 31st Drive, though it has gone through several name changes. And Fran Gallo, Tom's one surviving sibling, who lives in Bayside, Queens, still attends. "That's where I was baptized," recalls Tom. "I taught Sunday School there. One of the teachers, before I started teaching Sunday School, she used to take us by trolley out to Kissena Park in Flushing. We'd go out in the fields where there were daisies, and we'd pick some and bring them back to the church, for the altar. My parents were always Catholics really, because they never converted. They went to the Methodist Church, but they were never baptized Methodists. So until they died, they were Catholics."

CHAPTER TWO

Tommy Elmezzi, as he was known on Astoria's streets and playgrounds, often tagged along with his older brothers, Robert and Guido. At other times he was left behind, whenever his brothers and their friends took up some dangerous prank. This was the Roaring Twenties, when people's lives roared to the beat of a devil-may-care rhythm. Radio was in its infancy, television unknown. Young boys spent their free time outdoors, although most of the well-groomed parks New Yorkers now enjoy hadn't yet come into being. In Astoria back then, "outdoors" meant the steps outside a store, a construction site, even the dark, forbidding quietude under Hell Gate Bridge, where teenagers formulated grand schemes, pausing whenever a high-speed train roared overhead toward New England to the north or Manhattan's Penn Station and points south.

Tom's sister Fran recalls that Robert and Guido looked after Tommy, but she cites one instance where he wandered off. "One day Tommy didn't come home for dinner. My parents panicked and called the police, who finally found him meandering harmlessly around a building project." The incident also made an impression on Tommy, who remembers: "Sometimes I used to roam. In Astoria there was a big open field where the Triboro Bridge is now. It used to be farmland. Then they started to build what we called the Hundred Houses. I used to go into those places where they were building. I was always curious about how things were built. The biggest thing in my life as a child was being given an Erector Set for Christmas. I was crazy for that; I loved it. Even today I look to see what Erector Sets are like compared with what we had. We didn't get many toys, though, especially later, in the Depression. We didn't pass around gifts the way people do today. People today, they don't know anything about the Depression or what we went through. We had cardboard in our shoes. We'd have them resoled and resoled until you couldn't do it anymore. People today can't believe it."

Then there was the carnival site on property that is now LaGuardia Airport. Tom used to walk—not ride, he didn't own a bike—eight miles each way to prowl the fairgrounds. He was fascinated by the gypsies who held forth at the booths, telling fortunes and selling wares. He admits they scared him half to death.

The carnival property also served as a launching pad for small planes, which in those days provided entertainment more than transportation. In the 1920s the wealthy could afford to indulge themselves with plane rides to nowhere. Stunt pilots (including Charles Lindbergh) performed for the masses, and Lindbergh himself earned $25,000 for the first nonstop trip between New York and Paris. The best Tom's family could manage was piling into a taxi together, riding to the carnival area, and watching others take off. A pre-teen intrigued by the mechanics of aircraft, Tom little imagined what a world traveler he would someday become.

Automobiles were luxuries for the working-class Elmezzis. They didn't own one until the end of the decade. At the peak of the economy, just before the stock-market crash, Joseph was able to afford a 1928 Studebaker, then a hot item.

Few neighborhood swimming pools existed back then—the magnificent pool in Astoria Park wasn't built until 1936, by Robert Moses—but the rivers were relatively clean, so the boys did their swimming in the East River. Guido would sometimes swim to Manhattan and back, leaving his brothers on the Astoria shore. Guido in particular was a rambunctious youth, "a wanderer," as Tom recalls. He took off from home once and surfaced sometime later on an oil tanker. No one was surprised. Tom tells the story of Guido's putting Limburger cheese behind the radiator in elementary school, filling the halls with a unique Continental scent and infuriating Miss Hayes, the principal, and Miss Kaiser, the aptly named student disciplinarian. "My father didn't do anything to him. He never laid a hand on us, never ever. He just said, 'You can't *do* these things.' "

For his own part, Tom was well behaved in class. He attended P.S. 7 through grade 6, next P.S. 126 through grade 8, and William Cullen Bryant High, from which he graduated in three years. It would seem that Tom inherited different genes than Guido. Fran, although 10 years younger than her brother, was impressed with his conscientiousness: "Tommy was quiet and very studious. Always a good student." Jeanne, Tom's wife, agrees with her sister-in-law, with one caveat: "Tom was a good student, but he's always been a terrible speller."

Actually, spelling wasn't Tom's only problem in school. At Bryant High his history teacher went on sabbatical to be replaced for one semester by a drop-dead-gorgeous substitute named Miss Weston. She might have represented Tom's hormonal rite-of-passage, since for any student to remember the name of his substitute teacher after more than 70 years speaks volumes. Of course there may be another reason for the sharpness of the memory: After a semester of love-struck daydreaming, Miss Weston brought Tom back to earth by giving him an F. Nothing can dampen a young man's ardor for his favorite teacher faster than getting flunked. Tommy made quick amends, scoring 100 on the New York State Regents Exam and thus neutralizing his failing grade.

Tom graduated high school in 1932 at the age of 17. Though he planned to go to college—the only one of his siblings to do so—he also needed to go to work. The Depression had begun, and times were hard. "At that time, City College was a real good school. My parents, they never stopped me from bettering myself, but they could never do anything to help me, either. So I had to get a job." Luckily, Tom had two possible mentors. One was a rotogravure technician at one of the now-defunct New York newspapers—Tom thinks it was the *Tribune*—and he offered to get Tom in there. The other was a neighborhood pal of Robert and Guido named Richard John Ritchie, who went by his middle name. John, born in 1908, was head of his peer group, an outdoorsy type, gifted athlete and natural leader who played quarterback for the Astoria Willows, a local football team that traveled to New Jersey and Connecticut for games and once even scrimmaged against the mighty Chicago Bears, George Halas' Monsters of the Midway, losing by a single touchdown. Among the Elmezzi boys, Robert was the nearest to John Ritchie in age and was also his closest friend; he became manager of the Willows. Tommy was the team's water boy, welcome at games because he toted the pail to and fro during timeouts. At other times, especially when he was younger, Tom wasn't included when the older boys were heading off. "I'd try to follow, and my brother would turn around, throw me a quarter and yell, 'Get outa here!' So I'd go to the Astoria Theater, on Grand Avenue and Steinway Street. For a quarter you could see a movie and a stage show, with burlesque!"

The late John Ritchie's daughter, Joan Ritchie Silleck, tells of her father's demonstrating his youthful prowess by leaping over burning fires and encouraging others to follow. "They'd go out fighting to settle grievances," Joan recalls. But the combat was never serious; there were no Sharks and Jets in Astoria, and the boys didn't carry switchblades.

"There was a store near us," Tom says, "that sold vegetables and cold cuts and things like that. You had to go up three or four steps to go in, and in the summer, those steps were a good place to hang out. My brothers and John would hang around there, and whenever I could, I'd go over there, too." During the summer after his junior year, John talked with Tom about his plans for the future. John was 23 and already working as chief chemist in the Loft's Candy Co. laboratory. He offered to help Tom get a job at the company. Tom weighed the newspaper business vs. the sweets business, the *Tribune* vs. Loft's, and decided to throw in his lot with John Ritchie.

The Loft's Candy factory was on Vernon Ave. in Long Island City, a largely industrial neighborhood just south of Astoria. It made virtually all the candies, ice cream and other sweets that supplied the network of some 200 Loft's stores (including its subsidiary Mirror and Happiness stores), which extended as far south as New Orleans. "Some stores sold just candy, some had soda fountains, and some had restaurants," remembers Tom. "That's how we got in trouble—we had a high investment in brick and mortar, big overhead to maintain. At that time in the East, the only real competition we had was Schaeffer. Other than them, we were the kings of the industry. But the setup was too costly, and then the Depression came. Our competitors like Barricini started putting in all these hole-in-the-wall places. If our store was here, costing maybe $300 a month, they'd put one in across the street for $25 or $30 a month. On that basis, we couldn't compete. That was the beginning of the demise of Loft's Candy."

Tom started at Loft's at the age of 16, helping to make chocolate under the direction of Superintendent Heller and Supervisor Lowery. Even though he was just an apprentice, he was put in charge of three candy refining machines, rolling devices called enrobers, which have long since become dinosaurs of the confectionary art. Two of Tom's colleagues had three rollers apiece to operate, and when Tom cleaned his at the end of the day, much as one would rinse off the dinner dishes, his friends were upset because it meant they'd be expected to do the same. The Elmezzi work ethic made itself evident early.

By fall, Tom had moved into the lab to work with his mentor. "John's main job was coming up with flavoring. We had big storerooms and freezers down in the basement, where we'd keep the ice cream and the chocolate. In July we'd be making chocolate for Thanksgiving, and right after Christmas we'd be making it for Valentine's Day and Easter. We'd store the crude chocolate and then put it into different molds to make the different candies. We also had to do a lot of testing, to check the formulation of all the different products. Dark chocolate, light chocolate, Swiss chocolate. They take different amounts of sugar, milk, oils. We made the chocolate from scratch. We got the beans, crushed them, put them in heaters and then colanders that kept the chocolate mass moving back and forth, getting all the oils and the residue of the nuts. After that we added other oils, milk, and other liquids. From there it went to what we called a three-roller, that made it smooth, and then to a five-roller, that made it smoother yet. We had 50-pound containers that came off the five-roller, and we'd send them down to cold storage. Well, we had to test it at all different stages. Check the fat content, the sugar content, maybe add a little starch, depending on what we were making. We had maraschino cherries coated with chocolate—we tested those for sulfur content. We tested the ice cream, too. I used to run down to the ice cream plant, get different samples, run back to the lab and check them out. Check the fat, the sugar content, and the density. At that time there was a high fat content in ice cream, not like it is today. It's like water now, compared to what we made. Our ice cream had 19% butterfat. Now, the law is 11%, so you could make almost twice as much of today's ice cream from the stuff we were making then.

"Every morning, the chairman would come in. His name was Charles Guth, and we'd bring him the specialty of the day. Guth was a diabetic, but he loved everything that was bad for his disease. He loved sweets. He loved butter. So we'd bring him the day's special—for example, we used to make something called caramel parley, a caramel-nut-chocolate-covered thing, a wonderful candy. I think we sold three pounds of it for 99 cents. We'd bring him a sample, and he'd say 'No, no, no, you've got to make it sweeter,' or whatever. Then what we'd do, we'd wait a couple of hours and bring him the same sample. 'Oh, that's good.' See, Guth was a businessman. He was a shrewd man; he saw the future. But you can't have a businessman telling the technician what to do. It would have been different if I had brought him the same sample and he said, 'Wait a minute, this tastes exactly the same, what's going on here?' But Guth didn't really know what he was doing when it came to taste."

Nowadays, few people remember the name Loft's Candy. But consumers around the world know and love another product that came out of John Ritchie and Tom Elmezzi's lab in 1931: the modern incarnation of Pepsi-Cola.

CHAPTER THREE

The rise of the company we know as PepsiCo, Inc. was complicated and conflict-ridden during the 1930s, when Tom Elmezzi's career was beginning. This book will not follow every bend in the road—every proxy fight, every lawsuit, every shady corporate move. Such details have little bearing on Tom's story. But to understand Tom's role, one must travel back in time to the dawn of what later came to be called "The Cola Wars."

Sometime in the 1890s, a pharmacist named Caleb Bradham invented a new drink and served the first glass at the soda fountain of his store in New Bern, North Carolina. Bradham enjoyed coming up with soft drinks for his friends, and this one had medicinal properties, as did countless other beverages created during the 19th century. The most famous and enduring of these, of course, is Coca-Cola, which had been invented in May, 1886 by John Styth Pemberton, an Atlanta druggist. The drink's name advertised its origins: Pemberton hoped to capitalize on growing awareness in Europe and the U.S. of the stimulative properties of two plants: the coca leaf, from South America, and the kola nut, widely used to make beverages in Africa. Luckily for him, Bradham steered clear of coca, which later caused Coke considerable grief, and the active ingredient was dropped from its formula in 1903. (Coke continues to use "spent" coca leaves as a flavoring agent.)

"Brad's drink," as his friends immediately dubbed it, blended sugar, vanilla, oils and spices with kola extract. Bradham conceived of it as a soothing drink that tasted good, a palliative for stomach distress. The name Pepsi, which Bradham was using by August 1898, is derived from pepsin, a component enzyme, already recognized then as an antidote for indigestion. Today, Pepsi is marketed solely as an enjoyable beverage that confers vitality, sex appeal, and social cachet. Health considerations, other than slimness and sexiness, don't play any role in Pepsi or Coke ads these days. That's partly because of social reformers' efforts to discredit cola sodas as bad for teeth, loaded with caffeine, and even, when diet drinks were made with cyclamates, as carcinogenic—but mostly because of marketing and promotional imperatives. The image of a "Pepsi Generation" member doesn't include suffering from a stomachache.

In Pepsi's early years, Bradham emphasized the reverse. First, Pepsi made you feel better; second, it tasted good. As such, it was one of thousands of home remedies that dominated the medicinal landscape of the time. If one examines magazine or newspaper ads from the late Victorian era, it would seem that everyone not then a journalist was a medicine man. Any ailment (including those more imagined than real) could be remedied by Grandma Fishtail's Wonder Tonic, Harvey's Soothing Sarsparilla, or Aunt Cynthia's Purifying Potion. The names implied that the products had been prepared in your pantry by an adoring relative. Many such potions tasted like liquefied seaweed, but it didn't seem to matter. Whole catalogs were filled with pie-in-the-sky promises of permanent relief. Some even hinted at nourishment for the sin-sick soul as well. In fact the tonics did little or nothing to help anyone digest food or gain spiritual comfort. But they did dole out other sorts of comfort: Often they contained alcohol or other intoxicants such as cocaine.

The carbonated soft-drink industry fit into this marketplace for cure-alls, decades before the Food and Drug Administration began reining in the worst abusers. The mania was born of several factors: Mainstream medical science had not kept pace with the Industrial Revolution, a wave of new immigrants couldn't afford prescription drugs but would buy a cheap remedy by mail, and hard times had given rise to poor diets, heavy in lower-grade meats and starches. Coca-Cola became an immediate success by offering itself as a healthy alternative to liquor, thus riding the Bible Belt's revulsion to Demon Rum, a populist backlash that presaged Prohibition by three decades. The company sanctimoniously preached to the choir of teetotalers while keeping mum about the mind-altering properties of coca.

Its reticence on the matter ultimately didn't work, however. Articles began to appear in health journals about coca. Children's advocates were concerned the drink would become a substitute for orange juice or milk. It was argued in the company's defense that Pope Leo XIII, who lived to be 93, had lovingly imbibed a drink called *Vin Mariani*, blending Bordeaux wine and coca leaf, which was later identified as the grandfather of Coca-Cola. But the Pontiff's tastes and longevity couldn't quell the debate about the addictive properties of coca derivatives. Coke for decades was popularly known as "dope," and its ubiquitous red-and-white horse-drawn delivery vehicles as "dope wagons." When it finally dropped the active ingredient of coca from its formula, the company made no announcement.

Besides Coca-Cola, a few other companies that offered bottled relief for sundry ailments made fortunes before the turn of the century. Most who tried went bankrupt, either from business ineptitude or from having their tonics exposed as frauds. But Caleb Bradham was an honest pharmacist, and Pepsi proved immediately popular. In 1902 he hired someone to run his pharmacy and devoted himself exclusively to building his Pepsi business. In September, he filed an application to register Pepsi as a trademark and, in December, formed the Pepsi-Cola Company as a North Carolina corporation. At first he concocted the syrup in the back of his pharmacy and sold it exclusively to soda fountains. By 1909 the company was allied with 250 bottlers operating in 24 states. As had Coke, Pepsi benefited from anti-alcohol sentiment, which by 1910 was no longer a rural phenomenon based on religious fervor but rather a broad-based temperance movement linked to women's rights, because inebriation and spousal abuse often went hand in hand. The Volstead Act, the 18th Amendment to the Constitution that established Prohibition, was then less than a decade from passage.

Caleb Bradham's young company did just fine until after World War I. When war-mandated controls came down and sugar prices soared from around 5 cents a pound to 22 cents, Bradham found himself facing a dilemma. He needed raw sugar to make cola syrup, but he couldn't pass along astronomical price increases to Pepsi drinkers. Afraid of being priced out of the market altogether, he bought sugar contracts at 22 cents in 1920, only to see the price implode to below 3 cents in 1921. Pepsi was bankrupted, and Bradham was suddenly a country druggist again.

A Wall Street financier named Roy Megargel saved the company from disappearing altogether. Megargel put in his own capital and assumed control of everyday operations in 1923. He kept Pepsi alive, running it from a base in Richmond, Virginia. But Megargel always operated on a shoestring. Through the Twenties the company needed frequent injections of his personal funds, never once turning a profit, effectively going bankrupt a second time. Prohibition had in theory expanded the soft-drink market exponentially but hadn't helped Pepsi. Then the stock market self-destructed in 1929, and in June 1931, lacking further financial plasma from Megargel, Pepsi-Cola went bankrupt again. Only two independent bottlers remained in its network.

Enter one Charles G. Guth (pronounced as in Guthrie). More accurately, enter Guth's Loft Inc. Guth was a bullheaded opportunist with an instinct for the jugular vein. He'd capitalized on the death of founder George Loft, and the company's resulting management chaos and financial troubles (exacerbated by the stock-market crash), to gain Loft's presidency and control of its operations in 1930. He had been with the company only a year at the time.

Guth's sweet tooth contrasted with a not-very-sweet temperament. Loft's soda fountains and restaurants served Coca-Cola as their drink of choice, but in 1931 Guth, pointing out that Loft's nearly 200-store chain had bought an average of more than 31,000 gallons of Coke syrup per year over the previous three years, demanded a bulk purchase discount. Coke didn't see it his way. As a court in Delaware later remarked, "The controversy over price caused a sense of grievance on Guth's part," and he was determined to cut costs in a desperately bad economy. So he decided to dump Coca-Cola and find a substitute. He bought the trademark and formula of Coke's nominal rival, the recently bankrupted Pepsi-Cola. The trademark was what he wanted most, because Guth had already decided the formula would become history. Megargel's bankruptcy trustees had no choice but to sell out for a song. Megargel retained one-third of the shares in the new Pepsi-Cola Co., incorporated in Delaware on August 10, 1931, and was supposed to receive royalties that never materialized in any quantity. Two years later, disgusted, he sued Guth, and eventually settled for a flat payment, turning over his shares to Guth as part of the deal.

At this point John and Tom enter the picture in a way that seems beguilingly simple, yet changed their lives forever. Guth directed Ritchie, a 23-year-old self-taught chemist working with Elmezzi as his intern, to experiment with changes in Pepsi's formula. Guth didn't feel the drink as it was would satisfy his customers after years of Coca-Cola, so he told Ritchie, "Give me something new." So John and Tom set to work. "Guth wanted something like Coke but not Coke," Tom recalls. "That's why Pepsi has more of a citrus flavor, and Coke is more a spicy flavor. Guth wanted the citrus flavor. Cola drinks are all the same except the flavoring. So much sugar, so much caramel, so much acid, all that. Those are the same in all cola drinks. The difference is in the flavoring oils you put in. John did most of it; he was the head boy. I was the second fellow, learning at the same time. He'd try a batch with so much flavor X or flavor Y or flavor Z. I'm a citrus man myself, I like citrus flavors. So if we're trying one of those, I'd say, 'Let's put a little more of this in.' Not that I truly knew what I was doing." The flavoring oils, in other words, are the essence of a soft-drink formula. Which oils are used, and in what proportion, is a closely guarded secret. In Pepsi's case, as we shall see, the secret was astonishingly closely guarded.

"After we had some samples," Tom continues, "we'd test them. We'd get a few workers, three or four people, and put out a few samples and say, 'Which do you like?' They'd tell us and we'd make adjustments. And then we'd try it on Guth." The two technicians tinkered for about two weeks, hearing all the while they didn't quite have it yet, until they finally arrived at a blend Guth decided was "about right." This came as high praise from the demanding boss, whose generosity of spirit was always well concealed. For the next couple of years John and Tom continued to experiment, mainly with the goal of making Pepsi less sweet. "When we first came out with Pepsi, it had close to 15% sugar content. I mean, it was *sweet*. Everybody said so. It was like drinking sugar water; you couldn't taste anything but the sweetness. But that was how Guth liked it. At one point we brought it down to around 13% and took the samples to Guth. 'Oh, no, you can't do that.' O.K., we waited a while, brought him the same thing. 'That's better.' We were deceiving him, to be honest about it. You can't directly tell the boss 'You're wrong,' so we figured, well, find a way to do it. And we did. Nowadays, Pepsi has just about 11% sugar."

The drink created in the Loft's lab during those summer days of 1931 remained Pepsi's standard product for the next 20 years. It permanently altered the soft-drink universe, yet its two formulators were scarcely recognized for it. In books detailing this period in Pepsi's history, John is either ignored or briefly referred to as "Guth's chemist." Tom, who assisted him, shared joint possession of the formula for two decades, and exclusive possession for another 16 years, but isn't mentioned at all.

<hr />

It would be pleasant to write that after the invention of Pepsi's new formula, the fortunes of John Ritchie, Tom Elmezzi, Charles Guth, and the Pepsi-Cola Co. rose serenely together. Pleasant it would be, but wildly inaccurate. In fact, the eight years that followed the creation of modern Pepsi witnessed the equivalent of a marathon corporate food fight.

To summarize the tale, which will be examined in more detail below: The aftermath of Guth's 1930 takeover of Loft's included an unsuccessful decade-long effort by Coke to deprive Pepsi of the right to use "cola" in its name, beginning with the accusation that Guth was selling his new beverage in Loft's restaurants as Coca-Cola; Guth's abandonment of the daily conduct of Loft's declining business, because Pepsi had become so popular that he wanted to devote all his attention to it; a massive strike by Loft's employees, who held Guth incommunicado in his own office to dramatize their grievances; a raid by Guth upon Loft's treasury to finance Pepsi's expansion beyond Loft's-owned facilities; further deterioration of Loft's business; a Loft's lawsuit against Guth for misappropriating Loft's capital into an unauthorized outside business, that is, Pepsi; Guth's countersuit; success of the first action in a Delaware court, which saved Loft's from extinction and caused Guth's eventual departure from Pepsi; Loft's accusation that its own lawyers had overcharged it through contingency fees, later settled through negotiation; the rescue of a nearly bankrupt Loft's by Phoenix Securities Corporation in exchange for management control, this being Phoenix's speculative gamble on a successful outcome in *Loft's vs. Guth*, which by then had entered an appeal phase lasting two years; and finally, Loft's absorption into a new, Guth-less Pepsi-Cola, with a new management team headed by Walter S. Mack Jr., an erstwhile Phoenix executive who went on to run Pepsi ably for 10 years.

Against this background of uncertainty, corporate turmoil, and the Great Depression, Tom's real career as a production executive was beginning—not because he planned it that way, but because his natural skills as a technical problem-solver and diplomat led him in that direction. His immediate goal when he took his job at Loft's had been to put together money for college. He knew his father couldn't afford to send him, so the first dollars he earned went into a fund to pay City College of New York the $32 per credit that it then cost to matriculate there. After graduating from Bryant High in 1932, he went to work full-time for Loft's that summer, his workday lasting from 6:15 a.m. until 5:00. Even though Tom was employed in a chemistry lab, he started out at CCNY in electrical engineering, then transferred to New York University and switched to chemistry after his first year. He had to squeeze in his class hours at night and find time for homework after that. At least his work experience helped: "In the lab we were doing a lot of the things that they give you in chemistry classes," he says, "so I didn't have to do too much studying, because I'd been doing it all day long."

One saving grace was being able to live at home; another was public transportation. Tom had to trace a long, indirect route from the Loft's factory in Long Island City to City College's campus at 137th St. and Amsterdam Ave. He took the BMT to Times Square, then the Broadway line uptown some 95 blocks from there. He had to adapt to reading textbooks by the dim light of subway cars. And since teenage boys aren't fond of skipping meals, he also had to find the best spots for a nourishing, cheap dinner on the run. Fortunately for him, New York has always been loaded with such places. Still, it took him seven years to finish his education; he finally graduated from Pratt Institute in 1939 with a chemistry degree.

Tom's brothers, meanwhile, were also making their way in the world—one to a successful career, the other to an unfortunate end. "Robert went to mechanical school but he didn't go to college," says Tom. "He became a marine architect for Gibbs & Cox, which built the *United States*. He used to do all the piping work. But Guido went to war, to the Philippines. I don't really know what happened there, but I think he fell in with a Filipino girl. He was married, and when he came back home, one day just before Christmas, he committed suicide in his own house. His wife found him, called my brother, and my brother called my father, and my father called me. Guido had always been a wanderer. You'd be talking to him, and all of a sudden you'd say, 'Where's Guido?' Why, he's gone. Next thing we know, he's on a freighter somewhere. That's just the way he was.

<hr/>

While Tom was pursuing his chemistry degree, he got an education of another sort—in business and manufacturing. For the first couple of years after Guth introduced his new version of Pepsi in August, 1931, it hardly proved a success. Despite its captive market supplying syrup to Loft's soda fountains, the Pepsi-Cola Co. steadily lost money. Guth also sold Pepsi in 6-ounce bottles, but the little-known cola found few buyers. Guth went so far as to make an overture to Coca-Cola, asking if the giant cola company would be interested in buying his struggling upstart. In one of the greatest blunders in its history, Coke declined, no doubt figuring Pepsi would fail of its own accord.

Casting about for a gimmick to rescue the company, Guth in late 1933 seized upon the idea—whose idea it was is still a matter of dispute—of selling Pepsi in 12-oz. bottles for the same 5 cents that Coke charged for 6 oz. Almost as soon as the bottles hit the market, Guth knew he had a hit. Jobbers in New York who had ordered the first cases immediately began clamoring for more. Guth saw that enormous success was possible if he could expand at breakneck speed before other soft-drink companies, including Coke itself, matched his 12-oz., 5-cent bottle. He quickly made deals with several bottlers and bought plants outright in Montreal and Philadelphia. In New York, where he had been bottling under contract with Mavis Bottling Co. on 33rd St. in Long Island City, he cancelled the contract, leased the plant, and decided to turn it into a state-of-the-art bottling operation. But for the moment, that meant bottling Pepsi at the Loft's plant, and that posed problems for John Ritchie and Tom Elmezzi.

Vernon Ave. was a candy- and ice-cream-making site, so the young men had to adapt. "We put three little bottling machines in the garage, and they could fill 30 cases an hour. During those days, I did anything and everything they wanted me to do. I washed dirty bottles in a bathtub. A bathtub! I filled bottles. I capped bottles. I loaded trucks. You name it, I did it. There were only a couple of us, and I was the lucky fellow who got mixed up with the executives, and that's how I started to rise." On the 8th floor they set up a laboratory for mixing the flavoring oils. Three floors down, syrup was produced. Getting the oils to the 5th floor to blend with the syrup wasn't hard, but getting the combined product to Guth's three new bottling machines in the garage, there to be readied for distribution, demanded the creative imagination of youthful scientists—or budding production managers like Tom. The elevators in the building couldn't handle the bulk. Using cranes would have been overkill, not to mention expensive. The solution: run hoses out the 5th floor window and suck the concentrate hydraulically along the outside of the building. In 2003, Tom is the only man alive who remembers those hoses and their contribution to Pepsi's early success in New York, and he chuckles when he thinks of the Pepsi drinkers who had no idea of the unusual route the ingredients of their afternoon refresher had taken the day before.

"I have to give credit to Guth," says Tom. "He was a go-getter. He was a tough Prussian. And he was a man with great foresight." Once Pepsi began its astonishing climb to success, Guth immediately saw that volume was the key to the business. To achieve large sales volume, one needed both production and distribution. The key was an extensive network of bottlers nationwide—and even internationally, for Guth also pursued bottlers abroad from the beginning.

Bottling soft drinks might be compared to lighting the candles on a birthday cake. By the time you get that far, the most important work is done. For better or worse, the taste of the product is a fait accompli. But the bottling process is anything but trivial. It transforms a tasty product into a saleable commodity. Bottlers are to a soft-drink company what soldiers are to an army. During a "cola war," the company itself manufactures the artillery, but the bottler fires it.

In late 1934, Guth realized that franchised bottlers offered the best hope of the lightning expansion he wanted, so he divided the U.S. into four geographic regions, and Canada into two. He appointed a Territorial Representative for each region (except the Southwest, which never got an official representative) and sent them out to sign up bottlers with the incentive that for each case sold in his territory, the representative would receive 2 cents. The network grew fast, making millionaires of the territorial chiefs in the process.

Guth also pioneered in-house manufacture of bottle caps, boxes, and cases for packaging. Previously, soft-drink companies had outsourced these tasks to companies such as Crown, Cork & Seal. Guth even bought equipment so Pepsi could make its own labels, which from the earliest days had featured the distinctive curlicued name, always affixed at an acute angle from southwest to northeast.

During these early days, Tom undertook his first international troubleshooting mission—before his 20th birthday. "In 1933 I had to go to the bottling plant in Montreal because they had a problem with ring formation on the neck of the bottle. We didn't have the sophisticated water purification of today, and there was a breakdown of the caramel in the carbonated water, and that formed a ring. It wasn't harmful in any way, but we had to eliminate it, which we did by adjusting the formulation of those products, which had nothing to do with the flavor. Back in those days, I could take a bottle of Pepsi, and I could put it in a closet for 10 years, and it would taste the same. You can't do that with a tin can, and you can't do it today because you don't have pure sugar, you have fructose, which alters the taste, too."

In 1933, at the ripe age of 19, Tom was put in charge of production, and as the company expanded, his lifelong career of visiting plants around the world began in earnest. One such trip came in 1936, when he traveled to Havana to inspect a bottling operation Pepsi had just acquired. He was surprised to find the employees using slit trenches in lieu of restrooms. Tom, who had endured outdoor plumbing while growing up in Astoria, immediately had flush toilets installed at the plant. But he neglected one important step: going through Cuba's bureaucratic channels. The designated Cuban Labor Department official hadn't approved the changeover. Somebody had to sign off on such an improvement, and nobody had. So the toilets had to go, so to speak. The slit trenches were reinstated, and Tom learned his first big lesson in international corporate diplomacy: Always honor local customs, and never impose American values without preparing the ground first.

Tom faced a much tougher test after Guth made his most important move, aside from the 12-oz., 5-cent bottle: building a mammoth new bottling facility and sugar refinery in the Socony-Vacuum Building on the East River in

Long Island City. The property had originally belonged to the Rockefeller dynasty—in fact, John D. Rockefeller's office was still readily identifiable—but had long since been abandoned. As Milward Martin writes in *Twelve Full Ounces*: "There, he could have docks of his own where sugar boats direct from Cuba could unload, an enormous plant building ready for immediate use, and vast outdoor yardage where trucks could be maneuvered and garaged." Tom perfectly recalls the day in 1937 when he first saw the site. "Three of us went down there, Guth and me and a board member [Detroit bottler Walter Dawson], to look it over. There were acres of land for sale, used to be the old Rockefeller paint company. While we were there, he decided to buy it. The property was rather run-down. There were a lot of buildings, so we went to work. On one side of the property he decided to have a bottling plant, and he put in 10 new machines. There was no place anywhere in the world that had 10 machines going."

Such a move constituted an enormous gamble. Once a soft-drink brand gains acceptance and a bottler takes it on (this often means his having to retool operations), he has to worry both about his sales volume and about reliable supplies of syrup. Even a temporary interruption can be calamitous. By adding 10 bottling machines on the same site in Long Island City, all Pepsi-owned, Guth streamlined the production process. Everything was in one place. The product got out the door faster. At the same time, Guth had increased Pepsi's risk profile, because if syrup couldn't be made ready on time, regardless of the problem, Guth wouldn't merely have angry bottlers to assuage. He would have two separate divisions of his own company out of service, draining capital. Guth was hemorrhaging cash to lawyers just then, trying to fend off Loft's. But he was temperamentally ill-suited to half-measures, the kind of man who stared risk in the face and dared it to stare back. He forged ahead with the Long Island City plant, knowing full well that a lot can go wrong before product reaches bottle.

And things did go wrong. Tom, as a production manager in his early 20s, was not prepared for problems that arose with manufacture on that scale. One dilemma in particular demanded a combination of science and ingenuity. "We bought one million gallons of liquid sugar. It was delivered to us in the dead of winter. We had the trucks pick it up and bring it and dump it into this big tank we had built. In the meantime we had a smaller tank, 200,000 gallons, that was the original one that we used for our daily operation. Now, the main purpose of the big tank was that we'd have plenty of sugar available in the summertime to make the product.

"So one summer I was making concentrate over at the 33rd St. plant. We had 12 5,000-gallon tanks there. Some were used for syrup, some for concentrate, depending on where it was going. If it was going to the bottlers, it would go as syrup in tank trucks. And if it was going as concentrate, we'd put it in wooden barrels. Usually what I'd do is make a batch, check it, and then go out and check it again. This time, I noticed that it had gone down a few inches in the tank. I said, 'What the hell's happening here?' It was a concentrate tank. We happened to have an expert visiting at the time, William Hoodless of the

Pennsylvania Sugar Refining Company. Not knowing enough at the time, we had him climb into the tank to see what was wrong. Well, he nearly lost consciousness and we had to pull him out. There was carbon monoxide in there. It was spoiled, and the yeast had gotten into it. We tried to salvage what we could. Then I went to the sugar in the 200,000-gallon tank, and it was down, too. Same thing in the big tank.

"We called Mr. Hoodless and he told us what it was all about. This is what was happening. During the winter, it was cold, so everything was fine. But during the summer, you had the sunshine on that big tank all day long. The water in the liquid sugar would evaporate and adhere to the top of the tank. These were steel tanks, coated. At night it got cool and all that liquid up there would drip down and dilute the surface of the sugar, so the yeast could go to work on it. Pure sugar, yeast doesn't bother it. Can't touch it. But if it's less than 76% sugar, forget it, the yeast attacks.

"So what we did was, we reprocessed the sugar to salvage as much as we could. The rest we had to dump. Then we had to clean the tanks out, purify them again. And we tried an experiment with sterile lamps. I had become friendly with a fellow who was trying to sell me these ultraviolet tubes for purifying water. I never bought any for that. But we set up a stand with an ultraviolet lamp, and on the bottom I put an agar plate with some yeast on it. And I measured the distance, how far away the light could be and still kill the yeast. They were effective from six feet. So we installed ultraviolet lamps on the lids of the sugar tanks.

"But then I said, 'Well, they have to be cleaned. There'd be evaporation during the day, and that stuff got the lamps all dirty. How do you clean them?' So I went to Macy's and bought a six-foot rowboat. Once a day I'd put the boat in the tank and row around in there and wipe off the lamps. Later on, I figured out that I could cut holes in the top of the tank and put covers over each hole with a lamp attached. That way, I could just lift off the covers one by one, clean the lamps, and put them back."

———◆———

Thanks to the rapid growth of Guth's bottling network—by 1937, it was comprised of 313 domestic bottling franchises and five company-owned plants—Pepsi's sales continued to explode. This of course alarmed Coca-Cola, which soon attacked with every legal weapon it could muster, in hopes of crushing Pepsi as it had crushed so many other soft-drink startups. For some reason Coke failed to make the one move that Tom believes would have ended the cola wars before they really began: "All they had to do was come out with a 12-oz. bottle, and they would have destroyed us. If they had gone to a 12-oz. bottle, Pepsi wouldn't exist today." Instead, Coke first tried to prove that Guth was trying to pass off Pepsi as Coke in the Loft's stores, but aside from a few employees who had in fact left the Coke signs up, Pepsi showed that it was doing no such thing. Next, Coca-

Cola launched a flurry of trademark-infringement suits in the U.S. and abroad, claiming that the word "cola" was proprietary and thus could not be used by Pepsi. This tack had worked against countless smaller soft-drink makers that had been unable to defend themselves adequately. But against Pepsi's attorneys, Coke failed, with key courts ruling that "cola" was actually a generic term derived from "kola nut," a term that many companies had used, and that therefore Pepsi had every right to it. As Tom tells it: "Every case they brought, we beat them. We beat them in the U.S. We beat them in Canada. We even beat them before the English Privy Council. That's how cola became the generic term. Anyone can use the word cola today, but they couldn't before."

Guth's early victories against Coke, however, couldn't protect him from the consequences of his own behavior. As Loft's business withered and Pepsi boomed, Guth lost all interest in the candy company, and in the wake of a devastating strike brought on by his attempts to cut wages, he resigned his Loft's positions in 1935. What he didn't count on were determined Loft's executives and shareholders, who brought suit against him in December of that year, asking that all Guth's holdings in Pepsi-Cola be turned over to Loft's on the grounds that Guth had systematically and without authorization used Loft's capital, employees, equipment, and other assets to promote Pepsi's growth. It's one thing to abandon a dying business, but quite another to use that business's remaining cash to prop up another. Guth first counterattacked by means of a proxy fight to regain control of Loft's, but he lost. And the court case, *Loft's vs. Guth*, eventually decided by the Delaware Supreme Court, became a classic in the annals of corporate governance law. During the proceedings, none other than John Ritchie was summoned to testify, and he provided powerful ammunition about internal goings-on to back up Loft's claims. Guth was not amused. Even as the case was under appeal, Ritchie was summarily fired. Tom hadn't been a witness, but he was Ritchie's protégé, and as Tom maintains today, "Guth disliked Italians," so on Christmas Eve, 1937, Tom got the gate also, a victim of a) his friendship with Ritchie, b) guilt by association, and c) the fact that his surname ended in a vowel. Thus ended his six-year career at the age of 23—but not for long.

Justice sometimes has a way of prevailing. Two weeks later, Guth realized that his Prussian temper had gotten the better of his judgment. His supply of soft-drink concentrate had run out, and there was nobody around to recreate it, so the boss was forced to acknowledge that he'd axed the only two men who knew how. All was forgiven. Ritchie and Tom were rehired, unapologetic chickens allowed back into the coop by a self-interested fox. The two would outlast Guth at Pepsi-Cola by 12 and 35 years, respectively.

One of the key issues in the case was whether Guth had used Loft's employees to work on Pepsi business. To Guth, a born autocrat, this was a distinction without a difference: Both companies were his, and he could do with them what he liked. The court ultimately disagreed, ruling that Guth had in fact diverted many Loft's workers, including John and Tom, to build up a company that he owned virtually outright. But establishing that fact was not as simple as it might be today, because accounting practices were relatively primitive. When Tom went to work for Loft's in 1931, he would receive his pay in cash, in an envelope. There was no paycheck with a company's name emblazoned on it, nor any accompanying pay stub. There was no subtraction for Social Security—it didn't exist. Medical benefits? They didn't exist. 401(k) contributions? Many decades in the future. Taxes? Your own responsibility. Back then, one's boss did the arithmetic and handed out currency every couple of weeks, and that was it. The workers didn't care: In the 1930s, having a job was all that mattered. But to employers, one subtle advantage of such a system was that a worker might not be able to identify which company he was working for at any particular moment.

Tom laughs when he remembers his pay in the early days, and Guth's legendary stinginess. "When I began at Loft's, they paid 32 1/2 cents an hour. And every Christmas, when it was time for raises, Guth would stand in his door, and he'd say, "Tom?" And he'd hold up three fingers, like this. That meant a $3 raise — per week. Big deal! He had arthritis, so he couldn't hold up all five fingers, just three. But I didn't feel underpaid. You have to remember, this was the beginning of the Depression. Everybody was scrounging just to have a job. I was damn glad I didn't have to stand out in the wintertime and hope for work each day."

Loft's v. Guth dragged on in the appeal process, with new charges and countercharges, complaints about lawyers' fees, and with Loft's fortunes declining rapidly all the while. Through the late 1930s, Phoenix Securities

Corporation, a Wall Street investment firm, lent Loft's large sums to keep it afloat until the suit was decided. In return, Phoenix received guaranteed options to buy big blocks of Loft's stock at a low price. Phoenix was gambling that Loft's would win, a gamble that paid off handsomely. At Pepsi, meanwhile, certain shenanigans apparently were taking place. One day in 1939, Tom walked into his office and discovered that all his files had disappeared. For all he knew, or knows now, they had been dumped into the East River. Tom asked Guth's secretary what had happened. The obsequious Miss Castle proved to be the Rose Mary Woods of her generation by insisting she had no idea where the files had gone. "She doesn't know?" wondered Tom. "Did thieves come during the night? Could anyone so oblivious have survived this long as Guth's secretary?"

The drama reached its denouement when Loft's won the appeal in 1939. Guth was out, and Phoenix, according to its contract, had control of Loft's, and therefore Pepsi. Loft's was merged into Pepsi by a sort of financial alchemy, and Ritchie's and Tom's careers were saved in the bargain. Walter S. Mack Jr., vice-president of Phoenix, had become president of Pepsi-Cola in the wake of the original court decision in Loft's favor, and he now became chief executive as well. Loft's candy operation was spun off into a stand-alone company. As part of the merger agreement, James Carkner, late of Loft's Inc., became chairman of the new enterprise, and Joseph Murphy, from Phoenix-controlled United Cigar, became treasurer. Two law firms had prominently represented Loft's in the fight with Guth: Levian, Singer, & Neuburger, and Hays, Podell, & Shulman. They stayed on as Pepsi's counsel in a quasi-watchdog position, and several of their attorneys took board positions: one, Herbert Barnet, emerged as president of Pepsi 16 years later. But for now, everyone understood that Walter Mack was in charge.

And Mack, at least at first, proved more than up to the task. Perhaps his most vital move was to pump new life into Pepsi advertising. The centerpiece was the drink's new jingle, which made its debut in late 1939 and swept the nation in an event that Milward Martin calls "unique in American advertising history." Written by Alan Bradley Kent and Austen Herbert Croom-Johnson, the jingle was sung to the melody of the old English folk ditty "John Peel":

> *Pepsi-Cola hits the spot*
> *Twelve full ounces, that's a lot*
> *Twice as much for a nickel, too*
> *Pepsi-Cola is the drink for you.*

It proved so wildly popular that radio stations played it as entertainment rather than as advertising—and Americans, humming it happily to themselves, bought Pepsi in ever-increasing quantities.

━━◇━━

1939 proved to be a pivotal year for Tom as well. Since the year before he had been dating Jeanne Mastronardi, and on April 29 they were married at

Mt. Carmel Catholic Church in Astoria, on Newtown Ave. and 25th St.. Jeanne had lived at 1830 25th Road, across the street from the Elmezzi's final home in Astoria. Jeanne, who was four years older than Tom, had been born in Philadelphia. She was her parents' fourth child, following three brothers. Shortly before her birth in 1910, her father had been diagnosed with osteo-tuberculosis, which would claim his life three years later at age 38. Jeanne's mother needed to care for her husband, manage her family without a breadwinner's income or insurance benefits, and look after a new baby while raising three sons. It was too much for one person. Meanwhile, her mother's sister Lucia had always wanted children but had none. So Jeanne, at age 17 months, came to live with the Carras in Astoria. Later, Mrs. Mastronardi would ask for Jeanne to be returned home, but by then she didn't want to leave the only family she really knew, so Aunt Lucy said no to her sister. The Carras were Italian immigrants like the Elmezzis, but they had remained Roman Catholics.

Tom and Jeanne had gone to City College together, "but I got serious about her in 1938." Unfortunately, Jeanne's aunt and Tom's father found each other distinctly unattractive. Aunt Lucy became especially upset when her niece began seeing Joseph Elmezzi's son. According to Tom, Lucy "thought we were peasants." Jeanne has a milder way of putting it: "My aunt was just hoping I'd marry somebody who made more money than Tom did then." Tom was indeed making a very modest salary when he and Jeanne began dating. For his part, Joseph resented his neighbor's attitude and retained a chip on his shoulder toward Catholics generally. He didn't want his son to marry in a Catholic Church and especially didn't want to see him abandon Methodism to do so. Jeanne thinks there may have been another reason for the bad blood: Joseph and Jeanne's uncle Gaetano were both amateur vintners. They bought grapes in bulk and patiently prepared wine for personal consumption. But while Gaetano's cellar kept the wine at a perfect temperature, so his homegrown formula preserved its body and flavor for months on end; Joseph's tended to turn sour after a few weeks. But Tom insists the grapes of wrath had nothing to do with Joseph's bitterness?

In any case, the marriage proved a bittersweet occasion. Tom was confirmed into Catholicism shortly before the wedding, which proved the last straw for Joseph, who stayed home in protest. This meant Tom's mother Maria had to stay home, too, and an already uncomfortable family situation became a schism. Jeanne acknowledges that she always resented her father-in-law's cold shoulder on her wedding day. That feeling persisted even after she learned that when her mother-in-law lay on her deathbed in 1955, Maria Elmezzi conceded that staying home from the wedding had been a mistake. Women went along with their husbands in the 1930s, which Jeanne understands. Jeanne also knows now that Maria, as her dying wish, urged Tom to "take care of Jeanne."

Tom and Jeanne moved to 2710 Newtown Ave. in Astoria, where they continued to live until 1953, when they moved to Great Neck, a bedroom community for New York City, just across the Nassau County line. Great Neck has long been well-to-do, known primarily as an enclave for Jews leaving the five boroughs after World War II in pursuit of greener lawns and cleaner air. More recently, Hispanics and Asians have settled there.

Tom, of course, proved Jeanne smarter than her aunt. He became a world traveler who speaks several languages, a colleague of corporate giants, a man who knew two U.S. Presidents and several foreign heads of state. He achieved success and considerable wealth—the archetypal self-made man. But he has always lived modestly—no one would ever describe him as *nouveau riche*. The only less appropriate description would be "peasant."

CHAPTER FOUR

Tom Elmezzi was only 24 when Walter Mack assumed control of Pepsi. Despite his youth and sparse business experience, he would come to play a vital role in meeting the first "Pepsi challenge" of the Mack era: balancing its responsibilities as a patriotic corporate citizen against its destiny to grow in the midst of a world war. Under Mack, Tom would also become worldwide head of production and foster Pepsi's development into a true multinational. As with his contribution to the creation of Pepsi's formula, he would never receive due public credit for his efforts.

"When the war came," says Tom, "the people from the Office of Price Administration showed up at our refinery in Long Island City and confiscated 40,000 tons of sugar. Now what do we do? We can't get any more sugar. How do we keep the bottlers going? Well, Walter Mack was another astute businessman. He was rich, married into the Lewisohn family, a rich family. And he was quite a politician. He knew a lot of people in Washington. Of course, he was a Republican, and FDR was President. But he had enough power to go down to Washington and make a deal. He got permission to buy all the surplus sugar that Mexico would sell us. Then he said, 'O.K., Tom, put up a plant down there and go to work.' So that's what I had to do."

The reason Mack wanted to build a refinery in Mexico is that Mexican sugar was subject to U.S. tariffs. But if the sugar were made into Pepsi syrup before crossing the border, the tariff wouldn't apply. Mack decided to put the plant in Monterrey, near the Texas border. He also told Tom to build a barrel-making facility next door, for shipping the syrup across the border. Tom headed for Monterrey in early 1942.

Just why Washington granted Pepsi a sugar exemption is unknown, but F.D.R.'s people may have been throwing Mack a bone. Coca-Cola had already been granted an exemption from sugar rationing in exchange for Coke's commitment to supply the military. Washington even went so far as to pay for transporting Coke's bottling facilities closer to bases and war theaters, wherever such help would guarantee that Coke could meet its well-publicized pledge of providing "every serviceman a Coke for five cents." Pepsi hadn't gotten anything like the same break. Being allowed to buy surplus Mexican sugar was its only concession during the war.

Coke has always practiced ingenious public relations, but this was one of its greatest coups ever. By promising to supply the armed forces, it captured the patriotic high ground and won effusive praise from Washington bureaucrats. World War II was a time of bond drives, U.S.O. tours by prominent stars, and schmaltzy films that appealed to red-white-and-blue fervor. Coca-Cola fit the model perfectly. The company showed up for every bond drive, every U.S.O. tour, and managed to get its red logo on screen in many a newsreel and movie.

Lost in the flag-waving was the fact that soldiers were paying the same nickel per dollar that draft dodgers paid, meanwhile earning a lot less. "Every serviceman a Coke for five cents" sounded noble, but what were the folks from Plum Street really offering except more of their product at the everyday market price? The best to be said about Coke's gesture is that it saddled the company with additional distribution costs, but those they surely recovered through increased sales. The government's direct assistance on the bottling side more than covered the higher costs anyway.

Marketing genius? You bet. Patriotic selflessness? Well.... Yet somehow Coca-Cola emerged from World War II as a national icon, its image comparable to Bob Hope, Betty Grable, and the Andrews Sisters. Why? For promising a huge allotment of its basic product, at full retail, to men and women in harm's way who deserved to get it gratis...all the while being subsidized by the government. Of course, had it seen fit to, Uncle Sam might have snatched up Coke's production at a bulk buyer's discount and dispensed soda to every soldier and sailor, calling it a "C-ration." But the F.D.R. administration had already granted Coke a unique concession on sugar, and it might reasonably have felt that asking taxpayers to foot the bill for free soft drinks was overkill. So instead of promising "Free Coke for our brave boys defending freedom," which would have been a truly generous and patriotic offer, Coke won a phenomenal public relations victory simply by pledging to make its product available wherever the boys were in action—a victory that helped it emerge from the war with an even more enormous lead in public acceptance and sales volume.

Meanwhile, Pepsi was struggling simply to come up with enough sugar to stay in the game, and Tom played a major role in that battle. He oversaw construction of the Monterrey refinery and the barrel-making plant, which involved an adventure of the sort that production chiefs of major companies don't usually have to undertake. The absorption-resistant oak needed for syrup barrels wasn't available at sea level near Monterrey. Surveyors determined that one had to climb 5,000 feet into the surrounding mountains to find trees of the right size and toughness. It was Tom's job to inspect the trees. If he found them suitable, they had to be cut into logs, which in turn had to be brought to ground level without killing anyone. The problem was that the only access to the mountain with the oak trees was a narrow path, wide enough for a person to walk or a burro to trudge, but a burro carrying a man on his back would have found turning corners too risky. There was no way around it: Tom had to inspect the trees, or the barrels used to store the syrup might have leaked, given off an intrusive taste, or failed to resist moisture sufficiently.

Climbing the path, Tom didn't dare to look down at the precipices that fell away from the narrow path. He simply held on to the tail of the little animal moping along ahead of him, hoping all the while that the burro sniffing at his coveralls from behind had somebody loyal holding onto his tail, too. It was a one-mile climb, and if that doesn't sound like a lot, try it some afternoon under a Mexican sun, on the edge of a cliff, wearing a backpack and slogging between two incontinent beasts of burden.

Tom finally reached the top after several hours with two companions and three burros. As it turned out, the surveyor had done his homework right: The trees were perfect. Before they could become barrels, though, Tom had to supervise the construction of a 5,000-foot chute, down which the logs would be carried by gravity and a little luck. It all worked, and the mountain-climbing experience would stand him in good stead 17 years later in another Latin American venue.

But Tom's problems weren't over once the refinery and barrel-making plant began production. "I spent a lot of time putting that plant together and buying the sugar. Then we took the sugar and made syrup out of it by adding acid and caramel so it was no longer sugar. Every night I sent ninety-six 50-gallon barrels across the border to our warehouse. We'd distribute it to the bottlers, and they'd add the concentrate, what we called the 10-X. You couldn't use the syrup we brought in for anything else. But the U.S. government said, 'Hey, what are you doing there?' Because there was a 51-cent tax on every hundred pounds of sugar. They accused me of sending sugar across the border. I said, 'No, it's not sugar, it's syrup.'"

Customs officials were not convinced, and they took Pepsi to court in Laredo, Texas, charging tariff evasion. If the case had stood up, Pepsi would have had to pay the unpaid duties plus hefty fines, not to mention the publicity disaster that would have resulted from being convicted of such a charge during a war. But under Tom's direction, Pepsi's lawyers were able to show that the product crossing the Rio Grande contained flavorings that made it syrup, not sugar. Furthermore, they established this distinction without giving away any secrets in the courtroom, just in case Coke had spies in the gallery. The company was exonerated. The Monterrey plant only operated for a couple of years, because, as Tom remembers, "Other influential people in Mexico got the same idea about exporting the surplus sugar, and they depleted the surplus pretty damn fast. But it was enough to help us get through the war."

Similar maneuvers allowed Tom to keep the big Long Island City plant in operation. The government was confiscating raw sugar. "We had a 10,000-ton bin, and they took all that. But I also had a million-gallon tank of liquid sugar. Before they came back for that, I brought in tank trucks with caramel color, and we pumped that into the tank. Instead of having liquid sugar, now we had sugar with caramel, so it wasn't sugar any more, and they couldn't take it. You've got to stay one step ahead."

Other compromises were necessary during the war, a few of which strained the consciences of the compromisers. Even with Mack's success in obtaining Mexican sugar, supplies were tight. Pepsi's Iron Exchange plant in Marquette, on Michigan's Upper Peninsula, belonged to the Michigan Sugar Company. The plant was geared to producing sugar with a 95% purity factor, that being the government's peacetime mandate. But in wartime, 95% purity wasn't attainable, at least not in quantities required to operate Iron Exchange profitably. Tom had lower-grade sugar brought in from Louisiana to skirt the requirement. The plant also sometimes substituted honey for sugar. It was called "making do" in wartime.

In another far-off locale, the Philippines, Tom had to go even further to stay one step ahead during the war. In 1942, General Douglas MacArthur, having been overwhelmed by a Japanese onslaught, left the Philippines for Australia. Before he decamped, MacArthur made his famous pledge to the besieged Filipinos, "I shall return." Return he did, in 1944. And as U.S. troops reconquered the islands, Pepsi was preparing a shipment of more than 4,000 cases. "The fellow who took the 4,000 cases over was named George Anadale," remembers Tom. "He was married to a Japanese girl. And he started business in the Philippines for us. We gave the franchise to a Pepsi V.P., but Anadale was in charge of sales, distribution, everything. He was the head honcho."

Tom first traveled to the Philippines right after the war, and Pepsi soon built a bottling plant. But the nation had a high tariff on concentrated flavorings. "We had an attorney there named Bert Sabido," recalls Tom, "whose father was a senator in the Congress." He said, 'Tom, we're paying a lot of money for these imported oils. Anything we can do about it?' I said, 'Offhand, I dunno, but I'll see when I get home.' When I got back I talked to a couple of the suppliers, and they said, 'Well, we can make what we call "fourfold." That's when you take four pounds of the stuff and distill it down into one.' Which they did. So from then on, instead of importing, say, eight drums, I only had to import two. And pay tax on those two. And that was really the first step toward Diet Pepsi, because

I used the same concentrated oils when I made the Diet Pepsi formula."

While overseeing the construction in Monterrey, Tom commuted from New York for a time, but later moved into the Ancira Hotel for three months. Jeanne accompanied him for the first half of that time, then went home to Astoria. Tom didn't want to appear a carpetbagging gringo, and besides, he was a little homesick, so he assimilated into the life of the town, spending Saturday nights at the hotel bar (frequented by Americans) and Sundays with Jeanne at the local bullfight (frequented by everybody). There was even some danger that he would go dangerously native by being drafted into the Mexican army. "The working papers I had were called a *Forma Cinco*, a Form Five. That gave the Mexican government the right to draft me if they wanted. So for a while, I was marching on the square, practicing and drilling. But I came pretty damn close to the army saying, 'Boop, we're taking you!' Fortunately I was covered two ways: I could go in and out of the country whenever I wanted, and everyone at the border knew me, so I could have gotten out. And second, I was married and had the responsibility for my in-laws, so that helped me not to get drafted."

Around Monterrey Tom repeatedly encountered a shadowy American with whom he exchanged pleasantries about *los toros*, the war, and how to cope with the gastrointestinal consequences of drinking Mexican water. This was just another traveling Yankee, apparently, even though he seemed to pop up everywhere. Their meetings seemed coincidental, but in fact they weren't. At the hotel one night, as if in a scene from a Peter Lorre espionage film, the American casually suggested to Tom that Pepsi's syrup plant manager, a German named Jederman, had better be fired. The acquaintance didn't pursue the matter at that point — just tossed the idea out and then moved on — leaving Tom confused. The last thing he expected on a leisurely Saturday evening was getting advice on how to run his business, especially from a guy with no apparent credentials, and someone he'd only known socially. Fire Jederman? He was a valued colleague — reliable and conscientious — plus he had specific knowledge and skills Tom would have been hard-pressed to replicate in Monterrey. Fire him? Whatever for? And hold on a minute…how did this guy know who his plant manager was in the first place? Who had told him Herr Jederman worked for Pepsi, and why would he care?

At their next get-together Tom's friend flashed F.B.I. credentials, which showed he meant business. It turned out this was a matter of security and devotion to country. The wishes of J. Edgar Hoover had to be carried out. Jederman was a German. We were at war with Germany. So the F.B.I. had its eye on him, and he had to go, even though his activities, as far as Tom knew, were no more nefarious than the production of Pepsi syrup — and even though he was working in Mexico, a noncombatant in the war.

Had Tom's attractive history teacher, Miss Weston, ever discussed the Zimmerman Note at Bryant High? Tom couldn't remember. Woodrow Wilson's eventual rationale for bringing the United States into World War I in 1917 had been the interception of German Foreign Minister Zimmerman's message to

Mexico that sought its help in expanding the war into North America. The Germans knew that Mexico hated the U.S. then, and perhaps Mexico dreamed of getting Texas back. In any case, Hoover clearly saw any German on Mexican soil, especially one working for an American company, as a potential danger. So Jederman was fired, despite there being no evidence that he was linked to the Third Reich.

John Ritchie's son, Bob, who now lives in Charleston, South Carolina, recalls his father often telling of an intriguing incident that might have affected Jederman's fate. "My dad said the F.B.I. had been staking out the New York waterfront. You could almost see the Navy Yard from Pepsi's headquarters in Long Island City." The Feds had heard rumors about naval spy activity, and since German U-boats had been in the North Atlantic for a couple of years already, torpedoing passenger liners and passing within swimming distance of Cape Cod, it followed that the Nazis would be snooping out our naval capabilities along the coast. One German in particular had caught someone's eye.

So the G-men invaded Pepsi's Long Island City plant on December 8, 1941, even as we declared war on Germany. Their prey was a spy who, it turned out, had been in the U.S. since before World War I. Bob Ritchie continues, "Dad said they found this guy in Pepsi's office. It turned out he'd been there since the first war, not to help the Kaiser, but to gather intelligence in case a second war broke out." Could Jederman have been linked to this spy? Tom never knew.

Toward the end of the war, Tom traveled to Germany to help Pepsi begin operations there. Furnished with a visa that gave him the temporary rank of general, Tom first appointed a German-American, Karl Burkhardt, to run a plant in Schafenburg. "That was the first spot we were allowed to put a plant by the U.S. Army of Occupation. The plant was already there, but we brought the bottling equipment from the U.S. and started up there. Burkhardt was a big fellow, tall and hefty. He'd pick you up like nothing. A rough boy when he had to be. And he was astute in bottling operations because he used to run the Philippines plant. So we took him to Schafenburg. But then the Henniger Brewery wanted a franchise, and we gave it to them. They put their Pepsi plant in Frankfurt and turned the Schafenburg plant into a brewery. We wanted to work with franchisees, and we didn't want to run a bottling plant if we didn't have to. You have to remember, Coke had 110 bottling plants in Germany before the war, so they had a tremendous advantage over us. And that was true all over the world. I think the most we ever had in Germany was 10 or 15. I think that's down to two these days." Tom never called himself General Elmezzi, though he was entitled to do so while in Germany. But his status did allow him to live for several days in Kronberg Castle outside Frankfurt, where 125 years earlier a baby girl had been born who grew up to be Queen Victoria.

Tom's "rank" also helped him travel in the Russian zone. "They never gave me a hard time. The only time I had a problem was when I was leaving the country. The visa on my passport giving me general's rank had expired. I knew I would never get past the controls at the airport. Well, we had a guy named John

Meckler who was in charge of making sales to the PXs. He was an important cog in setting up Pepsi in Germany. He got the sales of Pepsi going while Karl was setting up Schafenburg. He had entrée everywhere: the PXs, the co-gen house, which is the club for the colonels and generals. He was like a little stick of dynamite—he was smaller than I am, but could he sell! Well, he knew the U.S. consul in Frankfurt. He went to the consul's house on a Sunday and got my passport stamped with a new date. I went to the airport on Monday morning. The customs guys couldn't figure out how I had gotten it stamped on a Sunday. I just said, "Go ask the consul." And they said, "Oh, go ahead." And that's how I left Germany.

By the end of the war, the young man from the streets of Astoria hadn't yet celebrated his 30th birthday, but he had helped Pepsi launch itself in Canada, Cuba, Germany, Mexico, and the Philippines. He would later open doors in Argentina, Australia, Bermuda, Brazil, Colombia, France, Ghana, Greece, Japan, Peru, South Africa, Spain, Turkey, Uruguay, and Venezuela. When asked how such a young man came to be entrusted with such responsibilities, Tom replies obliquely, implying that it was just because John Ritchie allowed it to happen. "John liked to travel, but only to Britain," Tom says. "He was Scottish. He wasn't interested in learning foreign languages. What he liked to do was play golf. But I enjoyed learning languages, and I was in the office on Saturdays, while John was on the golf course. He was a great guy, it's no criticism of him. I was just a go-getter." From the beginning of his career, Tom put in at least a six-day week, and sometimes seven. His work ethic was evident inside the office as early as the mid-1930s, when Pepsi Vice-President Walter Houston once found him on the phone at 10 p.m. discussing an emergency that had arisen regarding Pepsi's new operation in England in the middle of the European night.

⟹◆⟸

After the war, Pepsi's growth slowed noticeably. In an eerie reprise of Bradham's sugar price debacle after World War I, the company saw prices sky-rocket in comparable percentage terms from 2 cents a pound at the onset of World War II to 8 cents afterward. The reasons were easy to identify: the ending of wartime price controls, booming consumer demand as the servicemen returned home, women's move back into the kitchen from war factories, and gar-den-variety inflation. Pepsi had captured market share from Coke before the war with its 12-ounce bottle and its phenomenally successful advertising jingle, first launched shortly after Walter Mack's arrival as Pepsi president in 1939:

> *Pepsi-Cola hits the spot*
> *Twelve full ounces, that's a lot*
> *Twice as much for a nickel, too*
> *Pepsi-Cola is the drink for you.*

But with sugar prices soaring, the company now experienced a serious cost crunch. It was forced to pass along increases in its syrup price to bottlers, who winced, then passed the increase on to consumers. When they no longer were getting "twice as much for a nickel," they began to turn away, and Pepsi sales fell off in terms of both market share and simple volume. The numbers weren't pretty: In 1948, Pepsi sold 48 million cases, compared with 60 million in 1939, the first year of Mack's presidency. Pepsi's after-tax income in 1948 was a mere $3.2 million. Even more ominous, a poll of veterans taken that year by *American Legion Magazine* found Coca-Cola favored by 64 percent to Pepsi's 8 percent. Coke's World War II campaign was still bearing fruit. Reflecting all this, Pepsi's common stock was in the dumps. "Twelve full ounces" was obviously no longer enough to win a cola war.

For its part, Coke was also benefiting from help provided on Capitol Hill by an aggressive young congressman, then on its payroll, named Lyndon Baines Johnson. (It was O.K. then for congress people to work for companies whose interests they might be voting on.) L.B.J.'s path crossed Tom's one day in Greece while both were there "on business" after the war. "I ran into him in the elevator at the hotel. Coke had a lot of plants there before the war, so what he was doing was getting them started again where he could, or looking to build new ones." Of course, the two talked about cola, the topic they had most in common. Both were men who could get things done, though L.B.J. was more of a schmoozer than Tom. Otherwise, what a contrast! Here was a smallish city guy with conservative values from the paved streets of a liberal city discussing international soft-drink development with a drawling Texan from the hill country of a conservative state with crude habits and liberal values. At that point in their lives, both had already achieved a lot, and each would go farther. Johnson, always bent on becoming President, achieved it in tragic circumstances on November 22, 1963. Tom, meanwhile, was offered his own company's presidency, but refused it. Two such dissimilar men might never before have crossed paths in the soft-drink business.

In the years following the war, the huge Long Island City campus remained the focal point of Pepsi's operations. But Tom, when he wasn't globe-trotting, spent only mornings there. After lunch he operated out of Pepsi's new headquarters on West 57th Street in Manhattan. His daily shuttle illustrated the two hats Tom was now wearing: production guy and executive. He also had great influence over Pepsi's board, though that fact doesn't appear in any prospectus or book, and he himself didn't become a board member until 1963. As a holdover from the Loft's Candy days and a pivotal figure in Pepsi's dramatic growth, he had great credibility with Pepsi's directors, who had entered the boardroom through assorted doors: via Loft's, Phoenix, United Cigar, or, from 1939 on, Pepsi itself. Because of the fractious circumstances surrounding Pepsi's rebirth as a corporate entity in 1939, no member of the board trusted every other member. The board also had a high number of lawyers, some of them veterans of Loft's v. Guth, who had little or nothing to do with the actual operations of the company.

The divisions on the board often required the intercession of a trustworthy person from outside, and Tom often was that person. His devotion to the company was unquestioned and was undiluted by personal ambition.

By 1948 Pepsi's bottlers had lost confidence in the management team, in particular with Walter Mack. Tom became the pivot between Mack and his supporters on one side of the board, and Mack's undeclared foes (silently allied with the bottlers) on the other. Tom was a chemist, not a management specialist, but he had been around the soft-drink business long enough to know the need for keeping the company and the bottlers at arm's length. Allowing independent people to gain control of corporate operations was unthinkable, yet Tom found himself at a bottlers convention in Indiana, facing a disgruntled group speaking as one and demanding that Pepsi promote Domestic Sales Manager, Bill Durkee, to the top spot, replacing Mack.

Tom bristled. He had begun his career in a laboratory, but by 1948 he was spending half his time in an office and thinking more like an executive. "Who are you to tell us who our president should be?" he argued. "That's a board decision." Tom liked Durkee and thought him capable, but he wasn't about to encourage the bottlers to throw their weight around. At the same time, he couldn't lose his temper. The bottlers had lost faith, a fact he and the board had to reckon with. These were independent contractors, self-interested men who assumed Pepsi existed for their benefit, not the other way around. They'd take a hike if they got angry enough.

Sales were down. That was the bottom line. Mack was a financial man, not a true salesman, even if nobody dared to say so to his face. In 1939, he had been the right captain to take over a ship in danger of sinking. But Pepsi now needed someone new, and Tom, who had been through all of modern Pepsi's ups and downs, would help engineer another transition. The era of Alfred Steele was about to begin.

CHAPTER FIVE

Alfred N. Steele was a vice-president of Coca-Cola in 1948, in charge of bottler sales. A native of Nashville, Steele had first joined Coke in 1945. His association with Chairman Robert Woodruff traced back to 1943, when as an account executive with D'Arcy Advertising in New York City, Steele handled Coca-Cola's account.

Steele was a colorful character who'd once managed a circus. He was known then for identifying more closely with the charlatans behind the tent than the elephants underneath it. Unapologetically, Steele brought the flair and situational ethics of the midway into the advertising business, which then depended heavily on radio as an outlet. Meanwhile he formed friendships with singer Morton Downey (who accepted a Coke sponsorship), with Downey's agent Sonny Werblin (later owner of the New York Jets football team), and with Coke's public relations representative Steve Hannagan, who was then engaged to actress Ann Sheridan, a glamour gal known as the "Oomph Girl."

Coke's Woodruff was by habit a reserved Southerner (he enjoyed his cocktails, but in private), yet Steele drew him into New York's café society nightlife, which Woodruff found he rather liked. With Steele as his escort, Woodruff hung out at chic spots like Toots Shor's, the Stork Club, and the 21 Club. This was Steele's natural milieu, but it was light years from Atlanta socially. Woodruff was something of a fish out of water in the Big Apple, but he took to the dynamic ad man, never mind that at Steele's favorite places, Coca-Cola was used primarily as a mixer. Meanwhile, D'Arcy's ad campaigns, faithful to Coke's straight-arrow image, always promoted it as a stand-alone beverage, the favorite of thirsty G.I.'s. A paradox? Maybe, but so what? Wasn't rum and Coke General Patton's favorite drink? No one ordered a rum and Pepsi during World War II.

Woodruff hired Steele away from D'Arcy and put him in charge of sales, with collateral authority over advertising and promotion. Woodruff may have regretted the move immediately. Steele's bottlers' conventions evoked memories of P.T. Barnum. He brought in Broadway singers, dancers, band music, and girls in grass skirts. He backslapped his way around Atlantic City with a presumptive friendliness that disarmed people—and led others to underestimate him. Steele's hail-fellow-well-met bonhomie masked an acute business sense. He was fizzing with intelligence, but was more of a people person than an egghead.

Woodruff was still operating out of company headquarters on Plum Street. Atlanta was then a provincial southern city with an eye to the past—if not the plantation town of the 19th century, certainly not the modern, pluralistic commercial hub we know today. Coke's corporate image mirrored the city's and the era's—traditional, conservative, with a hint of pompous gentility.

Woodruff's lifestyle extended from his business life, and invariably reflected the Old South of his father, legendary Coke Chairman Ernest Woodruff, not the New South of the company's future. His leisure pursuits included fox hunting on his plantation in southwest Georgia, called Ichauway, where Mrs. Woodruff was rarely in evidence and where an ensemble of Negro servants catered to his guests' every whim by day, then returned to their dormitory at night. Woodruff enjoyed golf with Bobby Jones and Dwight D. Eisenhower at Augusta National and kept up a close friendship with baseball great and Coke bottler Ty Cobb. Woodruff ran Coca-Cola according to his father's example, with reverence toward custom, a hesitancy to innovate, and unflinching confidence in Coke's preeminent standing.

But now he watched Steele, the magnetic showman he'd hired, padding his expense account, calling everyone "pal," and turning Coca-Cola's marketing regimen into a long-run Broadway extravaganza. Sales had picked up, but at no small cost, because Steele was a profligate executive who might spend two dollars to make two. He paid lip service to controlling expenses, wasn't well organized, and for all his marketing dynamism, was easily distracted by wine, women, and song. His New York friend Hannagan called him "Tent Pole," a dual reference to his circus days and his virility.

In one egregious episode, with his wife home at the time, Steele brought a call girl to Atlanta and had her paged over the loudspeaker system as "Mrs. Steele." This was malapropos in Atlanta, where adultery wasn't necessarily frowned on, but flaunting it was seen as ungallant. In a second disaster, Steele organized a convention around a musical comedy revue, only to have the microphones fail. The actors flailed away for two hours in antic pantomime.

Woodruff was a careful executive whose career at Coca-Cola would span six decades. He recognized Steele as a mixed bag: The good Steele was selling more Coke, but the bad Steele conflicted with Southern manners and the company's traditional ways of conducting business. But Woodruff had brought Steele into the company, and Woodruff disliked firing people. So, like a Georgia farmer shepherding runaway livestock, Woodruff moved Steele to Atlanta, where he could keep a closer eye on him. The official thinking was that Steele would reform. Surely he'd learn that New York flamboyance didn't play in Atlanta.

But Steele was a big-city guy at heart, one who chafed under close supervision and who wasn't apt to change in his late 40s. Woodruff privately guessed Steele would quit, especially once he saw the hole-in-the-wall office Woodruff had picked out for him. He was also systematically shut out of company affairs: "no mail, no phone calls, no meetings," recalls one insider quoted in J.C. Louis and Harvey Yazijian's *The Cola Wars*. So when Walter Mack came calling with a job offer, Steele was ready. He joined the hated rival as a vice-president in 1949, taking a goodly number of Coke's key salespeople along for the ride. Meanwhile, Coke was still being offered in 6-ounce bottles only. That fact would give Al Steele a terrific opportunity to look good in his new spot. It was one he didn't pass up.

Tom and members of Pepsi's board well knew that Al Steele had come aboard to run the company. But Steele's ascent to the summit took a little time. Mack was still boss, and he had his own ideas about marketing. He thought of himself as an innovator, though some of his favorite techniques, such as skywriting ads, were not terribly fresh even then. As we shall see later, Mack was still trying to establish a niche in the soft-drink business when he was past 80, and he enlisted Tom in the effort. So in 1949, he was far from ready to surrender the reins, Steele or no Steele.

But as a financial man with a top-down approach to business, Mack couldn't relate to the disgruntled bottlers. He was a well-connected upper-class scion who'd married into New York's prominent Lewisohn family. But bottlers were scattered around the country, many in rural locations, so few circulated in Mack's Wall Street and Washington milieus. Mack's high-echelon contacts were helpful only to the extent Pepsi needed investment banking advice or regulatory concessions, not priority items in 1949. Tom knew this disconnect was Mack's fatal flaw and that Pepsi's meager sales numbers were proof.

For a short while, Steele settled for running the sales operation. But soon he made it clear he wanted full power to run the company, and the board, fed up with Pepsi's declining fortunes, backed him. He was named president, with Mack kicked upstairs to chairman. Mack was denied day-to-day control, so in 1950 he resigned. The transition was complete. Tom was pleased for Pepsi's sake, though he suspected his cherished 20-year business association with John Ritchie might soon end.

Tom was close to both Steele and Ritchie, and knew a philosophical gulf existed between the men that might be unfordable. The issue was basic: Would Pepsi alter the formula that had been in place since 1931, respecting Steele's vision of a new soft-drink marketplace? Or would the company do things Coke's way and honor the status quo?

Steele, possibly chastened by criticism of his personal conduct at Coke, wasted no time as Pepsi's president, determined as he was to reverse the negative sales trend and create a new image for the product. In 1950, many Americans saw Pepsi as too sweet — "bellywash" was the term used by marketing insiders — and too closely identified with lower-income consumers, especially minorities. Al Steele was no elitist, but his marketing intuition told him a consumer revolution was just beginning, and that Pepsi drinkers hadn't gotten the news yet. As Steele put it, he had to get Pepsi "out of the kitchen and into the living room."

"Living room" meant something different to Steele than it would to a realtor or furniture salesman. It was a marketing term, evoking an archetypal '50s family gathering spot with a television set. This was the era of *Reader's Digest*, Little League, Chevrolets, and *Father Knows Best*. Steele imagined upwardly mobile Americans hunkered down around the tube, loving *I Love Lucy*, safe from the Red menace, babies booming and dreams coming true through enlightened consumerism. Steele seemed to spend more time talking than thinking, but he could analyze marketing trends in his sleep. He wanted a change in Pepsi's formula, and knew exactly what his chemist had to do: reduce the sugar content and make the drink more tart, less caloric, more "with it"—conforming to a modern shopper's health consciousness. Saving on sugar also meant more profit, but Steele's overriding goal was capturing market share from Coca-Cola by competing in its upscale market segment, while still offering more soda for the money. To do that, Steele needed a new taste he could promote to the hilt.

Tom remembers the moment: "He asked me and John to go to lunch. We went to a restaurant on 56th Street, a popular spot that's no longer there. And he said to John that he'd like to change the formula to go with an advertising gimmick, which was lower calories. John insisted on not changing the formula. Well, Steele was a marketing and sales guy. He saw an opportunity and wanted to know how to go about getting it done, and he didn't want anybody to get in his way. So he said, 'John, I want to change the formula. Can it or can it not be done?' 'It cannot be done.' 'Why?' 'Well, it's gonna change the flavor.'"

John Ritchie had been around for nearly 20 years. He remembered the early days, especially the changeover in the Pepsi formula from a cola emphasis to the more citrus-y flavor. He was proud that his altered blend had brought Pepsi-Cola out of bankruptcy. It had been the signature moment of his career. Ritchie also thought more like a Coca-Cola executive: Go with the tried and true over the untested. Besides, between 1949 and 1951 he and Tom had gradually lowered Pepsi's calorie count from the sugary mix favored by Charles Guth to a more moderate taste, though it had never approached Coke's tartness. Ritchie thought Steele was going too far.

Steele responded by holding out an olive branch, maybe hoping flattery would carry the day. He put Ritchie in charge of all Pepsi laboratories worldwide, and promoted Tom to vice-president for operations. Here Steele was being consistent; throughout his business career he had appealed to subordinates by first honoring them, then trusting them to shelve their doubts and hop on his bandwagon.

But John Ritchie didn't lack self-esteem. He and Steele simply had a fundamental difference about soft-drink formulas, and the impasse couldn't be finessed. Or as Tom puts it, "How can you tell the CEO no?" So in 1951, Ritchie quit. To replace him in the labs, Steele tapped chemistry professor Steve Galvin of Rutgers University, a choice that revealed Steele's vision for the future. Al Steele, salesman and promoter, would thereafter concentrate on those priorities and leave chemistry to the professional chemists.

In a sense, Steele was one of the pioneers of the Information Age. He was one of the first to intuit that television would be more than a leisure-time alternative to golf or gardening; it would provide a road map for economic trends. Steele knew that Pepsi's fortunes, plus those of other consumer non-durable producers, would rise or fall less on product quality than on marketing hyperbole. In 1900 Pepsi had been a stomach soother; now Steele was determined to remake it as a path to upward mobility. He planned to emphasize social status, using TV as his primary medium. John Ritchie was a man of the past in the new promotional paradigm, so he had to go.

Remarkably, at this point Tom told his friend and mentor that he would follow him out the door. It was quite a gesture. Tom was no longer Ritchie's protégé; he had long since established his own turf at Pepsi. Furthermore, he liked

Al Steele, had welcomed him two years earlier, and was already in his confidence. In fact, Tom and Steele had hit it off to an extent that belied their polar-opposite backgrounds in the business. For Tom, though, the overriding factor was a sense of personal loyalty and gratitude. He stood ready to forfeit seniority and job security to stay with Ritchie. "I said, 'John, what do you want to do? Because whatever you want to do, I'll do. You want to leave? We leave.' And John said, 'Are you crazy? No, no, no.' He wouldn't even think of that. By no means." For Ritchie, as with Tom, relationships came first. No doubt he'd have made Tom the same offer had their positions been reversed. So Tom stayed at Pepsi, and Ritchie, even as he moved on to competitor Cantrell & Cochrane (makers of C&C Cola), kept their friendship alive for the rest of his years.

Tom remade Pepsi's formula to fit Steele's new advertising slogan, "The light refreshment." He won't say just what he did, other than reduce the sugar content to cut some calories. "I altered the taste," is all he will reveal on the subject. "When you take something out, you have to put something back. So you add different essential oils, and you have to know what you're doing, which one will create what effect." But two facts can be stated with certainty: The new Pepsi, propelled by its new image, was successful beyond anyone's—except perhaps Steele's—imaginings. And from 1951 until Tom left the company in 1969, he was the only person on earth who knew how to make it.

Tom recalls seeing Al Steele in the office "100% more often" than he'd seen Walter Mack. Steele always had a "Hi, pal, anything you need?" at the ready.

Tom says Steele was "always friendly" on a personal basis, though "he could be ruthless."

He also entwined his personal life with the company's affairs in flamboyant style. By 1954, Steele had been divorced for the second time. One night he flew to Las Vegas with a 50-ish woman he'd been seeing for a while. She had an unmistakable air of glamour, an eye tilted toward the nearest camera, and a veritable warehouse of stylish clothes. Friends hadn't been aware of their plans. Their children from previous marriages knew nothing. The couple slipped into town without fanfare. By the next day, papers had picked up the story. Al Steele and actress Joan Crawford had been married on the spur of the moment. It was his third marriage, her fourth. They left shortly afterward for a honeymoon in Paris.

Crawford, of course, was much more than an actress; she was a movie star in the grand old style. Originally a dancer, Lucille LeSueur combined charisma, just enough acting talent, a new Hollywood name, and considerable self-promotional skills into a stellar film career, one that skyrocketed just as "talkies" arrived in the late 1920s. It peaked in the '30s, a decade that saw her marry actor Franchot Tone (husband number two) and carry on a love affair with Clark Gable. In the '30s she also represented Coca-Cola, which specialized in celebrity endorsements. By the onset of World War II, her star had lost some luster. Though divorced from Tone, Crawford began adopting children, eventually taking in four. This was evidently an image-building strategy designed to mesh with the ethic of selflessness that prevailed during the war. It worked at first: Crawford won an Oscar in 1945 for her role as a woman with a hateful daughter in *Mildred Pierce*. The cruel irony of this triumph only became evident after her death, when oldest daughter Christina's 1979 tell-all book, *Mommie Dearest*, presented Crawford as an abusive alcoholic who'd used Christina and her three siblings as pawns in a Hollywood publicity campaign.

Occasional films followed, but by the 1950s, Crawford was middle-aged and her acting career largely over. A realist who still craved attention, she stood ready to face the limelight again, but in a new role: corporate wife. And what more perfect métier for Joan than a cola company? It sold a product she already knew well, and as Mrs. Alfred N. Steele, Crawford could live as she had in her glory years.

As it turned out, Al Steele and Joan Crawford were as perfectly matched as a mogul and a movie queen could be. Steele had the showman's gift and the business savvy; Crawford had the ready-for-the-camera public relations aura. Both had made considerable money by 1954, and both were spendthrifts. So they apparently adopted a newlywed covenant not to let glamour and celebrity get in the way of work, stuck to it, and worked hard. But they never made much effort to get their spending under control. It seems astounding in this era of corporate chieftains cashing in their hundreds of millions in stock options, but Al Steele needed his salary to live every week, and he never owned much Pepsi stock—considerably less, in fact, than Tom did. That's remarkable, especially considering that after 20 years on the job, Tom hadn't accumulated a single share of Pepsi. His first block came on Steele's initiative. A CEO doing something generous for a subordinate that he didn't do for himself—could anything illustrate more clearly the difference in business ethos from that time to this? Crawford, a Pepsi board member, never owned much stock either. She badly needed the salary Pepsi paid her after Steele died, while she remained on the board. Al and Joan always required cash flow.

When the Steeles arrived in Paris for their honeymoon, Tom was there, because Pepsi had other business to conduct in France. Love and marriage didn't dictate Steele's agenda. He used Crawford as a special travel companion/business partner, with emphasis on the business side. In Rome, where her old movies were still popular (new American films weren't distributed overseas quickly in the 1950s), Joan drew crowds as if she'd never left the silver screen, which gratified her ego. That was fine with Al Steele, because the adulation was good for Pepsi.

If, as in Rome, the occasion was the opening of a new bottling plant, Joan was the star of the show. But Tom was always there, too, and he and Jeanne typically occupied a room in the same hotel. Tom often filled roles outside the normal corporate routine. He held Joan's passport for a while. He was summoned to offer comments on the hat she was planning to wear on any given day. Because Joan liked Tom, he had ample opportunity to observe her transformations from disheveled early-morning hausfrau to midday glamour girl. "You wouldn't believe the difference," he recalls. "In the morning she looked like a wreck. Then she'd put her makeup on, do her hair, and magically the Hollywood star reappeared."

Joan never surrendered the prerogatives of stardom. Once, in a Buenos Aires hotel, she lost a front tooth at 2:30 a.m. Crawford called for Tom, who together with a Pepsi attorney managed to locate an all-night Argentine dentist for her. Things worked out, but Tom never figured out how her tooth could have come out at 2:30, why she needed him and a lawyer to find a dentist, or whether she put the tooth under her pillow afterward.

Jeanne says she had been a Joan Crawford fan decades before she and Joan met. When reality set in, Jeanne found herself traveling with a middle-aged executive's wife she later described as "a man's lady." That was Jeanne's polite way of saying Joan was a flirt. Crawford would have taken it as a compliment. Jeanne does warmly recall Pepsi parties at 21, where she joined Tom, Al, Joan, and Joan's friend Martha Raye, among other celebrities. "They had parties there all the time," she says, her use of the third person perhaps betraying the hostility she has felt for Pepsi since Tom's departure.

Tom rode with the Steeles on the company jet, a Fokker, to one Washington sales meeting. The Fokker had replaced a Learjet that apparently no longer satisfied the boss. Al Steele had returned to his extravagant Coca-Cola ways. He and Joan bought a Manhattan apartment and furnished it all in white. The centerpiece was a precious rug that no visitor, no matter how high-placed or famous, was allowed to step on without removing his or her shoes. Tom helped his boss furnish the midtown Xanadu, once again proving himself a most versatile worldwide production chief.

Steele adored the good life, and he cashed in every day. He was extravagant, yes, but never selfish, so his underlings loved him. Steele saw spending money as a validation of one's optimism and a reminder to strive for one's goals. In that spirit, Pepsi's headquarters at 57th Street, first occupied during the postwar Mack years, seemed cramped by the late '50s, and was too pedestrian for Steele's tastes anyway. He wanted more room, and a more prominent address befitting Pepsi's renaissance. There was no shortage of rental space in Manhattan, but Steele decided to build Pepsi a new home from the ground up at 500 Park Ave. The idea typified Steele's think-big style more than any other. From its ground-level glass doors to the penthouse suites on the 12th floor, the new headquarters would be class all the way, adding cachet to the company's image even as Steele sought the same for the beverage itself.

The new offices (Pepsi took occupancy in 1960) also added a feather to the executive headdress of Thomas D. Elmezzi, whose daily routine, when he wasn't overseas, became the following: pickup at his home in Great Neck at 6:00 a.m. and ride to Long Island City, where he worked until 9:30; drive to his suite at 500 Park Ave., labor until 4:00; back to Long Island City until 7:00 or 8:00; finally home. His ever-efficient secretary Joan Daley Blanc kept track of Tom's messages while he was en route from one office to the other.

Tom worked every Saturday to boot, so his driver, John Pursino, who'd started with Pepsi in Long Island City as a bookkeeper, picked up a lot of overtime pay. One wonders when John found time to spend the money, though. He lived in Massapequa, then an hour's drive from Great Neck; thus his normal workday began at 5:00 a.m. and ended at 9:00 p.m. Pursino, now retired and still living on Long Island, was never heard to complain. Tom's work ethic must have rubbed off on his employees.

Business was booming—from 1950 to 1960, sales climbed 185%, and profits soared from $1,271,000 to $14,180,000, growth much more rapid than the industry's as a whole. In Steele's first five years, Pepsi's market share rose from 21% to 35%. The Coke-Pepsi sales ratio sank from 5—1 to 3—1 by mid-decade. By 1959, it was down to 2—1. Coke had been forced to adopt a 12-ounce bottle at last, and Steele's promotional steamroller had come up with "The Sociables," a campaign that added snob appeal to upward mobility as its guiding tenet. Pepsi was now officially out of the kitchen and into the living room.

The confidence of Pepsi's independent bottlers, so low a few years before, soared in the 1950s. Steele was an evangelist at bottling conventions, grabbing the podium and loudly proclaiming, "You men have been driving Fords. Now you'll have Cadillacs." The bottlers responded with standing ovations. Steele was their man, a welcome contrast to Walter Mack. He told them they'd become millionaires, and they believed him. Many did, in fact. Under Steele, bottlers were sought out for advice on advertising and promotion, which under Mack would have been unthinkable. The bottlers rubber-stamped most ideas, despite having to share costs all the way. The old jingle, "Twice as much for a nickel, too," had been shelved, of course, because Pepsi now cost a dime. But it was replaced by the equally effective "Twice as much and better, too." By the time Coke switched to a 12-ounce bottle in 1958, Pepsi had gained market share for seven years, appealing simultaneously to the consumer's waistline and wallet. Steele had been right.

Then, on April 18, 1959, just after completing a worldwide tour to promote "The Sociables," Al Steele died of a heart attack in New York City at the age of 57. Tom got the news from Jeanne upon returning from church that Sunday morning. "I just said, 'Ohhhhh,'" he remembers, shaking his head sadly. "Steele was such a great man." His death came a few months before Pepsi scored an enormous publicity coup in Moscow, where Vice-President Richard Nixon and Soviet Premier Nikita Khruschev, strolling through a trade fair, drank Pepsi together just after having engaged in their famous "Kitchen Debate." Khruschev pronounced Pepsi "very refreshing," and pictures of him with a Pepsi cup were beamed all over the world. Steele also did not live to see Pepsi move into 500 Park Ave., the headquarters he had built as an exclamation point to his success and high profile.

<hr>

Tom was busy overseas during much of 1959. With Steele gone, he knew the task of maintaining Pepsi's growth abroad would fall on him and on the director of international sales, Donald M. Kendall—the man who had engineered the Nixon-Khruschev Pepsi-fest. Tom didn't foresee that Kendall, who had joined the company out of the Navy in 1946 and was married to the daughter of a Pepsi board member, would later orchestrate his departure from the company.

But the signs were there. By 1959 Tom had already begun to doubt that Kendall had his best interests at heart. He had noticed that the man always took center stage in photographs, wanted his own way all the time, and acted as if he were Tom's boss when in fact he wasn't. Kendall was a hard-driving executive, talented and highly successful, but also nakedly ambitious. People either loved him or hated him. And Tom, by putting his feelings aside and pursuing what he thought was best for the company, unwittingly prepared the ground for his own ouster.

CHAPTER SIX

"From 1951 on," Tom says, "I had the formula to myself. Nobody else had it. I carried it with me. Everywhere I went I mixed the flavors. I had to travel all over the world doing that, and just to get the flavors into some of these countries was a chore. I had a lot of good fellows to help me out. But the board of directors never asked me, 'What's the formula? Where's the formula?' I don't know if they thought I had a copy locked away somewhere. Could be. Nobody ever asked me. If I had been killed in a plane crash, it would have been tough luck, as far as the formula was concerned."

It seems astounding now that a rapidly growing multinational company would entrust its most essential trade secret to one man who traveled constantly— especially in the 1950s, when intercontinental flight was riskier than it is today. The only logical explanation is that everyone at Pepsi assumed Tom had deposited the formula in a safe place, so they never bothered to make sure. And later in his career, as we shall see, when Tom knew his position was threatened by corporate infighting, he felt possession of the formula afforded him some security: "When you're dealing with rats, how do you protect yourself? I just kept quiet."

He kept going, too. Tom's sole knowledge of the formula meant that he was the only person would could mix the ingredients for Pepsi concentrate at plants around the world. At the same time, he was heavily involved in expanding Pepsi's territory by building new plants, often in far-off lands. These two tasks meant that he was on the road at least half the time.

"In Long Island City here, I'd mix up a batch of concentrate nearly every week. I started out with a 300-gallon tank, and at the end I had a 5,000-gallon tank. It was right outside my office. The materials would come in—I'd buy the flavors from different outfits. They would come in, and I'd put them into what we called the cold room. All the flavor was kept in the cold room until it was time to use it, cooled down to 40 degrees. When it was time to mix a batch, I'd go into the cold room, that's where the tank was. It was a big round vat, stainless steel, on the floor. We had an opening on the bottom, and we had a pump so we could pump it wherever we wanted. The cans of flavor weighed anywhere from 5 to 50 pounds. It would take me a couple hours to mix a 5,000-gallon batch. I could make one today; I could write down the mix right now. So I'd get the mixture all done, and I'd say, 'O.K., boys, it's all yours.'

"To protect the formula, what I'd do, I'd make the main batch, and then I'd make a partial batch on the side. That way the people at the plant couldn't tell how much I had used of each ingredient See, the guys would know how much of each ingredient we had on hand—X hundred pounds of this, X hundred of that, and so on. So if I just made a batch and left it at that, they could tell what went into that batch. But if I made a half-mixture as well, they wouldn't know what went into each batch. Then the next time, I would finish that batch and make another half-mixture. I was in control of the formula, and I wasn't going to let anybody else in the picture.

"Same at the overseas plants. Every concentrate plant I put up, and at the peak we had 21, when they needed flavoring, they'd tell me, 'We're low, you better get over and make some more.' Usually I'd make enough to last a few months, but it varied with the plant. I'd make a batch and a half, and that way the secret was safe.

"I didn't taste the flavor mixture, but every sample of concentrate made while I was there, I would taste. I would taste a bit of syrup, which had the sugar and water in it, and then they'd put it in the bottling plant and make the drink out of it, and we'd check it out, we'd test it to make sure it met all the standards, the acidity, the color, the homogenization. That was a tricky process. You've got eight ingredients that make up the flavor mix. The concentrate is made up of water, sugar, caramel coloring, and citric and phosphoric acid. That's an acid that's beneficial to the body, good for the teeth, and it helps balance the acidity of the product. You want to keep it as close to 3.2% acidity as possible. At the beginning we used gum arabic to make sure the essential oils were mixed properly. Then we put in machines called homogenizers and did away with the gum. It's just like milk, you've got to get it mixed so it doesn't separate. Why don't you have fat on the top of milk anymore? Because it goes through homogenizers. Machines with three pistons going continually. The liquid comes down a pipe and into the homogenizer, and the pistons pound it with 4,500 pounds of pressure. With Pepsi, the machines pound the flavoring oils into the sugar and water, breaking them down into smaller and smaller pieces so they won't separate again.

"In fact, at one point Coke called me and asked me if they could use caramel coloring to help them do the mixture. I had a patent on that. The caramel helps to emulsify the oils. The idea came from our lab, we had a few fellows down there who were quite astute. And we were the first to put in homogenizers. So when Coke put them in, they couldn't use caramel unless I gave them permission. They called me and I said, 'Fine, go ahead.' Gave them a letter and that was it. I was friendly with some of the Coke guys. There was no animosity. We didn't run the company. We were just doing what we were supposed to be doing. So if anybody needed help, I'd try to help them."

Tom points out that Pepsi now operates its entire global production by making concentrate in just two places: Puerto Rico and Cork, Ireland. So why did Pepsi once have concentrate plants spread all over the world? Because at the time the company was embarking on aggressive international expansion, nations wanted to make sure they kept as much production and employment as possible within their borders. They were happy to welcome Pepsi-Cola; the growth of communications, in particular the export of American films and television, had combined with improved long-distance air travel to widen consumers' horizons. If Pepsi appeared in a movie or TV program distributed abroad, local viewers wanted to try it. Other publicity stunts like luring Khruschev to quaff Pepsi in front of the cameras in Moscow brought the drink global attention.

The Elmezzi family around 1920. From left: Guido, Angelina, Maria, Tom, Giuseppe, and Robert.

Tom's parents—Maria and Giuseppe Elmezzi, around 1940.

Tom's grandparents, Franchesca and Damiano Battaglia with a niece, in Italy around 1910.

Gaetano and Lucia Carra—Jeanne's aunt and uncle who raised her.

Brother Guido, during World War II.

Al Steele

Kissing Miss America in 1964.

Tom dancing at Roy Wilson's wedding in 1966 in Mexico City.

Alongside Peter Warren in the 1960s.

Tom with Joan Crawford in Argentina.

Opening the Bermuda plant in 1957.

Norman Heller, at the time of the launch of Diet Pepsi.

Relaxing in the office gym.

Tom and Jeanne (back row, center) at the wedding of Carl and Nancy Gallo in 1980. Tom's oldest brother Robert is standing on the far left.

Carl Gallo in the late 1990s.

Tom and Jeanne in 1996.

Tom with the JET Foundation board members in 2003. From the left are Lynn Grossman, President of the Jet Foundation and Tom's financial advisor; Al Larosa, Tom's accountant; Tom; Steve Saft, Tom's legal advisor and Secretary of the Foundation; and Nivia Pedroza, Tom's personal assistant and VP of Operations for the Foundation.

Thomas Elmezzi—The man who kept the secret.

But sometimes Pepsi would sign a deal to supply a bottler with concentrate made elsewhere, only to have the host country reverse field and demand that the company produce locally. For example, says Tom, "We had to put a plant in France. The government said, 'You gotta put a plant in.' Then the Spanish government got the same idea. What are you going to do? You always have to try to keep ahead of yourself to make sure the bottlers have syrup. We didn't have the experience Coke had, because they had all this stuff before the war. So I was running around establishing all these places. But it wasn't easy, you have to get all kinds of permits and see how you can get raw materials. I can tell you, I had my troubles. People have no idea what it meant to do that, the loneliness, the sickness, the headaches to get these things done. Altogether we were in about 100 countries. But we didn't have plants in all of them. We supplied different places from England. Same with France. From Kenya we supplied most of Africa. In South America, we had plants in Rio, Montevideo, and Buenos Aires. One in Mexico City. In the U.S. we had four. At one point I had 21 concentrate plants. Now they're down to two."

Throughout this period of rapid expansion, one of Tom's closest colleagues at Pepsi was a short, stocky Canadian with pronounced bulldog tendencies, William B. Forsythe. Walter Mack had originally hired him away from Coca-Cola in 1940 and put him in charge of Pepsi's export operation, a task Forsythe applied himself to with obsessive energy. He began by criss-crossing Central and South America and the West Indies, looking for good candidates to run bottling operations, and his success accounted for much of Pepsi's strong presence in those regions for decades. He nearly broke his heart striving to capture the English market for Pepsi, but never managed to overcome local lack of enthusiasm for soft drinks—perhaps because the English at the time were accustomed to drinking their beverages warm. But that was a rare failure for Forsythe. By 1954, when the export operation was incorporated as Pepsi-Cola International Inc. under the laws of Canada, it encompassed 118 bottling plants operating under Pepsi franchise in 52 countries. Two years later, when he retired, 149 plants were running in 61 countries.

Forsythe's personal resume was even more striking. In September 1939, the passenger liner *Athenia* took a torpedo from a German U-boat in the North Atlantic, and sank. Forsythe was on board, and he became a hero by risking his life to save others. He spent days drifting in a lifeboat before an American destroyer picked him and the other survivors up.

Then, in 1949, Tom says, "He and I were both going to Mexico one Wednesday. We were supposed to get on American Airlines Flight 156, I still remember, to Dallas. But I said to him, 'No, I'm not gonna go, I'll wait, there's other things I want to do.' He got on the plane. It crashed in Dallas and again, he saved people. He had a remarkable way of living. Once he went salmon fishing in Northern Canada and developed a toothache. He wouldn't give up his vacation, there were no dentists around, so what did he do? He took pliers out of his tackle box and yanked out the tooth. Then he went on fishing."

Tom well remembers his first trip to South Africa, in 1948. Jeanne came along for the ride. It took three days to get there on DC-2s and DC-3s, with stops in the Azores, Lisbon, Dakar, Monrovia, and Leopoldville in what was then the Belgian Congo. As Tom's plane came in for its landing in Johannesburg, he noticed a succession of long sand dunes on either side of the runway, extending as far as the eye could see. It was as if someone had built a desert on the outskirts of a large city. "What are those sand dunes all about?" Tom asked his first-class traveling companion, whom he hadn't officially met. "That's the residue of gold mines," came the reply. "The gold has been bled out and made into ingots. What you see is what's left." Tom then introduced himself and was surprised to discover that his informant was none other than Coca-Cola's local franchisee, Mr. Cohn, returning home from business in New York. It was the second time that year Tom had struck up a conversation with a stranger while many time zones from home, and that stranger had turned out to work for Coke. The first had been Representative Lyndon Johnson, in Athens.

Tom had embarked for Johannesburg because two brothers-in-law named Miller and Wilson, Americans married to South Africans with connections to a clothing-store dynasty, had decided they wanted to become Pepsi bottlers. They succeeded, but only after Tom flew in, made his own connections, and learned that he would have to build a concentrate plant near the bottling facility. He and Jeanne then left Johannesburg and flew north to Cairo by way of Nairobi. Both cities were part of Pepsi's international network at the time. Our globetrotting couple didn't expect to have to spend several nights en route in a fleabag hotel in the Sudan, but when their plane landed in Khartoum for a stopover, somebody discovered a part was missing. None of the local hardware stores happened to have it in stock. Jeanne was able to salvage a memento from her unplanned visit to Khartoum—a leather purse that she has never used in the 55 years since. She wasn't sure how well it was made, so she simply saved it as a souvenir. She smiles when recalling that trip: "I always felt the business about a missing part was an excuse. The pilot just wanted a rest."

Jeanne might have been right about the part. But in the jet age it's easy to forget the days when four-engine propeller airplanes circled the globe. Tom still shudders at the memory of one return trip from Johannesburg a few years later. After refueling in the Azores, his Constellation lost an engine, requiring a drop in altitude of 3,000 feet. A while later, just after reaching the point of no return, it lost a second engine. It couldn't afford to lose a third, or Tom's career would have ended somewhere in the broad Atlantic. The pilot managed to reach Bermuda, where everyone transferred to another plane and continued safely to New York.

Occasionally Tom's problems had to do with soft-drink parts, not airplane parts. Cairo, where Tom had been headed when his plane broke down in Khartoum, was home to Pepsi's largest bottling plant in the Middle East. A few years after the Sudan incident, Tom visited the Cairo plant, then flew on to London, only to find a message waiting for him to the effect that a certain

Egyptian jurist, known as a mufti, had decided that because Pepsi-Cola's formula included the enzyme pepsin, it didn't conform to Islamic laws and was therefore *verboten* for Egyptians. Tom had to fly back to Cairo (for some reason the telephone wouldn't do) and personally explain to the mufti that Pepsi had long since dispensed with pepsin, and the fact that the drink was still known as Pepsi-Cola had to do with the commercial value of brand-name labeling.

On Tom's first trip to Australia in the late '50s—another 3-day slog, with refueling stops in places like Fiji—he became seriously ill once he got to Sydney. "It could be a little scary at times," he says. "I knew no one. No one. The only place I knew was the hotel I was at. And I was sick as a dog. I didn't know what the hell to do. Who do you turn to? Finally I just went down to the desk and said, 'I don't feel so good, I'm gonna stay in my room,' and that was it. Fortunately I got better. And as you go along traveling, you learn by experience. You figure out where the American consul is, or the embassy. And in the course of events you meet people, or you meet someone who wants a bottling plant, and you have a discussion and you become a sort of acquaintance." On subsequent visits Tom kangarooed about the country, eventually establishing bottlers in Darwin, Perth, and Brisbane as well as the inevitable concentrate plant in Sydney.

In 1957, Tom went to Tokyo and met with Japanese Prime Minister Tanaka. Speaking perfect English, Tanaka-san's first question was: "Why do we need you when we have Coke?" Tom had heard that song before, of course, and would hear it again. But he was patient, recognizing that Japan, as with the Philippines, remained under American domination, and that the Japanese had long since learned it didn't serve their interests to resist overtures from U.S. corporations. So the concentrate plant was built.

Soon afterward, Tom and Jeanne visited Tokyo again. En route home in his usual first-class seat on Pan Am, Tom became aware of what sounded like an out-of-control, airborne day-care center operating in the adjoining coach cabin. He investigated. It seemed 18 Korean War orphans were traveling to Honolulu without chaperones; this was an immediate problem, because in those days Tokyo to Honolulu was a 12-hour flight. From Hawaii the tots were to somehow clear immigration and proceed to Washington, D.C., where adoptive parents were waiting to meet them for the first time. Apparently nobody thought to send along a babysitter, so the stewardesses had to fill this role on a rotating basis. This meant somebody else had to help out serving coffee, tea, and milk…not to mention other beverages. Guess who volunteered? Tom remembers having to put the brakes on one especially demanding passenger, then on about his fifth cocktail, who was wondering why Pan Am's usual prompt service had languished. With a blend of firmness and tact, Tom managed to persuade the gentleman that milk for Korean orphans took priority over more booze for an already well-lubricated businessman.

Bermuda was a hop-skip-and-a-jump by comparison. Pepsi and Tom were attracted to its proximity, and especially to the tax advantages enjoyed by

American companies that set up operations there. So long as profits earned in Bermuda were kept offshore, they weren't taxable at home. But Bermuda's a small island, and land isn't cheap, so American companies couldn't just bring in bulldozers and jackhammers at will. As it happened, an old fort built by the British in Somerset Parish had been abandoned. Tom doesn't recall how long it had been standing idle, but at least since the Spanish Armada gave up thoughts of reclaiming the island for Juan de Bermudez.

Now, imagination helps in building a worldwide soft-drink operation. Relatively few abandoned forts become concentrate factories. Growing up in Astoria, Tom had seen plenty of construction sites but relatively few gun turrets, and the only thing that resembled a moat in his neighborhood was the East River. But over a period of six months, he sized up the Somerset site, struck a deal with local authorities to permit conversion of the fort, and Pepsi built a plant. A photo shows Tom cutting the ribbon, surrounded by Pepsi executives and local dignitaries. The plant operated for 10 years before being moved to Puerto Rico.

By the late 1950s, coping with overseas laws and regulations sometimes steered Pepsi toward buying existing operations rather than setting up new ones. In Uruguay, for example, Pepsi opted to diversify by purchasing Paso de los Toros, a maker of tonic beverages. This brought Tom there in 1959 for another climb up the side of a Latin American mountain.

The bitter flavor in tonic comes from the peel of an orange. In Uruguay, orange groves happened to be located high along its border with Brazil, and they had to be inspected before Pepsi would O.K. the merger. Growing up in Queens, Tom hadn't ridden many horses, but at least he had climbed a 5,000-foot mountain in Mexico clinging to a burro's tail. This time, at least, there was enough room for a horse and rider. So when in Uruguay, do as the gauchos do: Pepsi's cowboy remembers riding along steep trails he hoped his mount had climbed at least once before. Fortunately, Tom had memorized the Spanish word for "whoa." He was struck with the crude implements used to remove the orange peels and leave behind juicy round pulps. The peels were kept, the fruit given away to grateful locals, and Pepsi-Cola soon owned Paso de los Toros. Tom and his traveling companion, Pepsi Financial Vice-President Louis Nufer, finished up their business in Uruguay and headed off to nearby Argentina, hoping to arrive in time for an evening meeting.

Buenos Aires is only an hour away by air, but by the time they reached Montevideo's airport, the last commercial flight had departed. So Tom commissioned a private plane. Then the fun began. Tom and Nufer were driven to a grassy runway on the outskirts of the city. There, the two men met a sorrowful-looking gentleman of swarthy aspect who they presumed was guarding the property. No one else was in evidence, so Tom asked the supposed watchman in Spanish, "Can you tell us where our pilot is?" "Si, Senor," came the reply, "I am the pilot. We are going to Buenos Aires right now." Tom gulped.

After a few anxious moments the tiny plane did get airborne. But as the only man who knew the Pepsi-Cola formula turned and looked back at vanishing terra firma, he noticed the cabin door had flown open. Small aircraft flying at relatively low altitudes don't have pressurized cabins, so Tom and Nufer were spared the indignity of being sucked out into the air. The pilot was unmoved by the occurrence. By the time they landed safely, the door had opened again, as if granting our two Phineas Foggs a spontaneous welcome to Argentine soil. Somehow they made their appointment on time.

Tom remembers more happily another air travel experience of around the same time. "We were flying a Strato-Cruiser to Europe. That's one of those bulky planes with a downstairs lounge for the first-class passengers. I knew the captain well, and he invited me up to the cockpit. Well, later on he got tired. He decided to take a nap. So he put the thing on autopilot and asked me, his passenger, to keep an ear out for messages from the ocean below." In those days, ships were placed strategically around the ocean to serve as communications stations for transatlantic flights passing overhead. "I actually made one of the contacts," says Tom, by now comfortable in his role as civilian volunteer at 35,000 feet.

Later in 1959 Tom found himself back in Argentina, where Pepsi still hoped to gain a foothold despite several unsuccessful prior efforts. By now he'd identified the problem; it reminded him of his Tokyo experience. The local bureaucracy was openly partial to Coca-Cola. But let's let Tom tell this one:

"I had a flavor supplier, an American guy by the name of John Cassulo. He was a deep-sea fisherman, and he was building a boat in Argentina. One day

I said to him, 'We've been trying to get into Argentina for years, but we can't seem to get in. They don't want us in there.' He says, 'If I call you, can you come down?' I say sure. He calls me on a Wednesday and says, 'Can you come tomorrow?' I say, 'I'll be on the plane.' So I go down there. I'm met by some gentleman, and we go to the hotel. Casullo calls me on Friday morning and says, 'Tonight we have a party to go to.' I say, 'Oh, O.K.' So this fellow who met me at the airport picks me up again and takes me to the party. We go to the party and meet a lot of different people — great, fine. And my friend says, 'Tom, we have a meeting with the President at 9:30 Monday morning.' The next morning I get up and get dressed, ready to meet the President. I go there and, unfortunately, the President's secretary, a little fellow like me but thinner than I am, starts giving me the third degree. Why Pepsi? We have Coke, and so on. I explain to him what it would mean, that by letting Pepsi in, so many more people would go to work, the different industries that would be affected, trucks, bottles, glass, advertising, promotion. So he says, 'Go see the Minister of Commerce. Unfortunately you won't be able to see the President." So I go to see the minister, and it's the guy who drove me in from the airport. I couldn't make head nor tail of this. We finish and he says, 'Look, I think there's possibilities, but you've gotta get an O.K. from the Central Bank.' I say, 'Where's the Central Bank?' He says, 'Across the street, down to this corner,' and so on. I go there, and the guy I was supposed to meet was the guy who gave the party. He says to me, 'Look, I have your application. You cannot tell me that you can't get some of this equipment here instead of importing it all. Why don't you look it over, see what you can get here, get what you can, and we'll O.K. it." And that's how we got into Argentina. All this was set up by Cassulo. I finalized it, but without him we wouldn't have done it. They were doing my friend John a favor. He was the type of guy that if you met him, you'd be happy with him. He was a liver of life.

"The irony of that one is that in 1961, I was with my wife, going to Argentina to open up my concentrate plant. And on the same plane along comes John's wife and this other friend of mine. I said, 'Where are you going?' She said, 'John is missing.' She didn't know the whole story at that point; she just knew he was gone. When she got there she found out he had taken the boat around to Peru to a fishing tournament. It was a foggy day and he insisted on going out. Some boat or ship hit him, I guess, because they found parts of his boat and his briefcase. The sharks must have gotten him and his crew.

"Anyway, Joan Crawford was there with everyone else; we had a nice opening at the plant, and Argentina was pretty good for a while."

At other times, socializing wasn't enough, and diplomats had to get involved. Pepsi's operation in Matanzas, Cuba, was threatened in 1959, soon after Fidel Castro came to power. Castro's predecessor, Fulgencio Batista, had pretty much left Pepsi alone, provided things were done according to Cuban rules and regulations, a lesson Tom had learned the hard way back in 1936. Now, Castro had decided that Pepsi was being used as a front by the C.I.A. More than that, its manager was a C.I.A. agent. Fidel had the man thrown in jail, finally releasing him only after intense diplomatic pressure.

There were also times when Tom carried the ball himself. In Turkey, for example, "The sales department tried for years to get us in, and they were unsuccessful." But in 1964, Tom thought he might have a partner who could get them in the door. "I found a bottler who was making juices. He had a fruit and vegetable operation on the other side of the Bosphorus in a town called Basra, a canning operation—he used to can foods in a crude way. Pepsi asked me to go down and look at the bottling plant in Istanbul. When I went in there I met an older man who looked a lot like my father; he had two sons. Their family name was Sipiolou. This was in Istanbul. I went around the place, and it was immaculate. I went to the bathrooms. I checked behind the stalls. I wanted to see what kind of a bottler he would make, a clean bottler or a dirty bottler. Then he took me to his place in Basra where he had this canning operation. We spent the night there and went over his whole operation. Came back, went to the plant again, and I said to the family, 'If I'm not back in six months, forget about it.' So I went to our salespeople and said, 'I think this is what we're gonna do.'

"Then I went to two other friends of mine who were flavor suppliers. They had been supplying me for years, and I had a lot of trust in them. I said, 'Now, how do we get things into Turkey?' Because you weren't allowed to import flavors. In the meantime, I had to figure out things like how we'd make caramel color over there. I had to get a cooking vat, and I had to get raw sugar. So I finally got that ordered. We were able to get that with fairly little trouble, because I told the Turks, 'If we put up a plant, we're gonna need people.' So they allowed it. But we needed flavors and they said, 'Go get local products.' Well, there were no local products. These oils come from all over the world, not from any one spot. Some come from Jamaica, some from Florida, some from Argentina, some from Italy. Take orange oil, for instance. If you take an orange and you squeeze the peel with a spoon, some liquid comes out. That's the pure oil. Now if you heat it out and mix it with water, you have to extract it again. You get back to the pure oil, but it's not as good as the first oil. We used to get orange oil mostly from Italy. Then you have the spice flavors and the different nuts that are used for spices. They come from different places again, as does the kola extract itself. So I had these friends and I said, 'O.K., this is what I need.' They got back to me that they'd work on it. Finally they found a way of bringing it all into Turkey, and I paid them. How they did it, I couldn't care less. Just get me the flavors. And they did, it all came through.

"In Spain, I had the same problem I had in Turkey. I didn't have all the materials. Again, I said to a couple of my suppliers, 'I don't care how you do it, but we have to have this plant in Spain.' Soon after that, we got the stuff over the Pyrenees into Madrid. And we used it. We'd say we bought it locally. Nobody knows where it came from, or how it got there. I used to have a suitcase, and I'd bring machinery parts with me. I'd say to the fellow that was supposed to be meeting me, 'You make sure the customs guy knows what the hell's going on when I come through.' When I got there, he goes, 'O.K., O.K., O.K., O.K.'

Never looked at a bag. I could've been carrying a bomb."

As successful as Pepsi was internationally from the 40s to the 60s, in recent decades it has lost considerable ground—and Tom has strong feelings about how that happened. "At the beginning, everything was going O.K. But the company didn't give the bottlers abroad the proper support, the support you need if you're going to build something," he says with a sigh. "Advertising. Promotion. If you want to succeed, you have to help others help you. If you don't give them that support, they don't have enough to fight the competition. That's the basic problem: How could you fight Coke if you don't get support? Like I said, before the war Coke had 110 bottling plants in Germany. We had none. How are you gonna fight that? You have to give your guys a hell of a lot of help and support. Maybe you're gonna lose a lot of money at the beginning, but you have to take the long view. Anyway, it's too late now. We lost it. We'll never recoup the international business.

"The other thing is, when the parent company gets into a country, they send a bunch of Americans down to oversee the plants, manage the plants, and they don't belong there. We didn't know anything about these countries, but we had people here who did know the bottling business, the ad business and the sales business. The idea was to send them over and give them a piece of territory, France or Spain or Germany, so they ran the show. But then what you have is a foreigner going into these countries where it'd be better to get a local guy to do the same thing. At less expense. Yes, we needed the initial aid and knowledge from the U.S. But as quickly as possible, you turn it over to local people. There was never an American running any of my plants. Always a local guy.

"I remember one time—in Italy we had a very good operator who was in charge, an Italian. But over him they sent this American. Moved his family there. Two months later they moved him back. That's tens of thousands of dollars wasted. I don't know what the hell happened, but there were several incidents like that. Of course, the fellow who goes overseas, he wants American schooling for his kids. He wants a car and a driver. You don't need that if you've got a local guy. I used to say all this inside the company. But you can't control the whole thing. Some of the things we do are right, and some are wrong. You can never be 100%."

Tom still believes passionately that when one is in Rome, one should do as Romans do—and hire Romans to do it. He also still refers to Pepsi as "we"— some 34 years after being ousted from the company.

CHAPTER SEVEN

Emmett O'Connell, who became president and chief operating officer after the death of Alfred Steele in 1959, wasn't a "Don Kendall man." His tenure as Pepsi's C.O.O. would prove to be short, but he found time to make his feelings clear to Tom on that score. Tom's duties did overlap with Kendall's, but in Pepsi's organizational chart, Kendall had responsibility for worldwide sales, Elmezzi for worldwide production. These were separate fiefdoms, and O'Connell meant for them to stay that way.

By 1959, though, Tom realized that Kendall wanted production brought under sales. Ostensibly this would streamline the operation and clarify accountability. But the change would have given Kendall total control over Pepsi's international operations. This was a defensible strategy in an M.B.A. textbook, but Pepsi's methods had never conformed to business school precepts. Quite the opposite, in fact—simply consider Tom circling the globe several times a year to make concentrate because he was the only man who knew Pepsi's formula.

O'Connell outranked both men, and he was opposed to any change, so Tom went about his travels in the post-Steele era with the comfort of the new boss's support. But in 1961 O'Connell died. His death, as sudden and unexpected as Steele's, left C.E.O. Herbert Barnet facing a dilemma: Who should be named president? Barnet, a lawyer, had been involved in the *Loft's v. Guth* litigation back in the 1930. He had returned to Pepsi after the war and was named president in 1955 and C.E.O. to succeed Steele. His primary function before the war had been safeguarding the interests of his law firm, serving as its representative on the board. When he came back, Barnet played watchdog for Pepsi, making sure everyone kept his nose clean, and wielded a red pencil over budget and expense overruns, which were always Steele's Achilles' heel. But Barnet stayed mostly in the background during the 1950s and did his job quietly. Unlike Guth and Mack, Steele eagerly delegated authority to subordinates, so Barnet was free to play cop while Steele expanded the business. Barnet's low-key ways dramatized the gulf at Pepsi between "inside" and "outside" men. Lawyers and financiers such as Mack and Barnet had to work alongside "sell-their-socks-off" marketers and salesmen like Steele and Kendall. When conflicts arose between the camps, Tom, neither an inside nor an outside guy, often held the balance of power, as he had during the transition from Mack to Steele, and as he would do again soon.

<hr/>

During the interregnum between O'Connell and Pepsi's next C.O.O., the company pulled off a major coup: launching a diet soda that handily beat the offering of its arch-rival.

The groundwork had been laid back in the 1950s. Having appointed Professor Steve Galvin of Rutgers to replace John Ritchie as director of laboratories,

Al Steele left him alone and concentrated on sales and marketing. Meanwhile, surveys suggested that Pepsi, to retain acceptance as a status beverage, had to go even further to satisfy a calorie-conscious populace. Because Galvin and Tom spoke the same language, they worked closely together with new combinations of oils to create a diet drink. By the early 1960s, a new question had emerged: What mix of oils is best suited to a drink using saccharin and cyclamates, which had much less of an aftertaste than other diet sodas that had been on the market since the 1940s?

The paradox of more Americans becoming more overweight yet more diet-conscious at the same time was steering soft-drink chemists aggressively toward sugar-free sodas. It was an extension of Steele's vision—an upscale consumer seeking refreshment not in conjunction with food ("out of the kitchen") but as a social lever ("into the living room"). It's hard to meet someone new in the kitchen, harder still if you're overweight—so the more people gained weight, the more they wanted to lose it.

Meanwhile, in Washington, Jackie Kennedy was First Lady. Jackie was anything but fat, and she presided over a social revolution that blended youth, glamour, and celebrity into what her husband's image-makers called the new Camelot. Cold War tensions overseas and civil rights tensions at home made daily headlines, but in the lives of ordinary Americans, both took a backseat to self-improvement. It might not have been what the New Frontier's media advisers had in mind with the Camelot metaphor, but if Jackie wore a certain dress, millions of women wanted to wear the same one. When John F. Kennedy went hatless at his inauguration, it virtually destroyed the hat-making business in the United States.

A new word entered the everyday lexicon: "vicarious." Women wanted to look like Jackie, and men wanted to spend the weekend with women like Jackie. It was the ideal time to bring a new product to market that might make someone look slimmer, seem smarter, feel younger, be sexier, and act cooler. Of course, Diet Pepsi, which the company introduced in 1963, hadn't been developed anticipating Camelot—it evolved from experimentation that predated the Kennedy years. In fact, Royal Crown Cola had come out first with such a drink, Diet Rite Cola, in 1960, and as J.C. Louis and Harvey Yazijian point out in *The Cola Wars*, it promptly grabbed 50% of diet soda sales. In 1963 Coke followed with Tab and Pepsi with Diet Patio Cola. That uninspired name was soon changed to Diet Pepsi, which by 1965 had nearly overtaken Diet Rite, while Coke languished badly in third place.

Making Diet Pepsi posed technical problems for Tom and his colleagues in the lab—and also led to a missed opportunity that Tom recalls with some amusement. In his own words: "You needed something so the oils would emulsify and mix like they should, and you have to make sure it won't separate later. You have to have something to hold it all together. The sugar helped a lot with that. So how to do it without sugar? What we did, we started with gum Arabic, heated it up, made a solution out of it, then we mixed the oils into that. It worked perfectly. So Diet Pepsi, I can say that the formula is mine, period.

"At first we used cyclamates. Then the government came along and said it caused cancer. I said 'Go to hell, it does not.' But they banned it, so we had to switch over to saccharine. The irony of that is I was working with a man on producing saccharine. We were going to build a plant and sell it to bottlers. He had a great method for making it, so it would have been a coup, I would have controlled the production of saccharine. We were all set to go, put up a plant, and I asked him to show me his patent. Turned out he didn't have one. Ohhhhh. I don't know what he was thinking, maybe it just never occurred to him. Someone else had bought the patent, the company that ended up making all the saccharine. We would have had a plant and nothing to do with it."

⋙◆⋘

Herb Barnet, low-key and unhappy in the limelight, was ill suited to be the operational head of a soft-drink company whose growth depended largely on hard-driving leadership and flashy publicity. The bottlers didn't particularly like him. So he had to find a replacement for O'Connell. Tom never sought the job, but he was an obvious candidate. He owned the respect and confidence of the bottlers, the trust of the board, and had no visible enemies inside the company. Nobody understood Pepsi's history, or its mission, better than he. So in

September 1963, Barnet asked Tom to accept the presidency of Pepsi-Cola. At age 48, the son of Italian immigrants stood at the threshold of a higher station in life than anyone could have imagined. It must have come as a surprise to Barnet when Tom declined his offer.

Tom saw the job of president as largely one of public relations, speech-making, and socializing. For an Al Steele, these tasks came as easily as breathing. Also, Steele had chosen the ultimate corporate wife, ex-movie-star Joan Crawford. Tom's life partner, on the other hand, disliked parties and didn't care for schmoozing with her husband's business acquaintances. A college graduate, one-time substitute teacher, and a distinctly attractive woman, Jeanne nonetheless was the un-Joan Crawford, one who wanted no part of the limelight. Tom knew that accepting the presidency would put his wife into an awkward position.

Then there was Tom's own personality. "I'm not a public speaker. I'm not looking for glamour. I'm an operations man. I like the nitty-gritty," he says. While certainly articulate, Tom isn't tall or imposing, and he felt he lacked the stage presence to "wow 'em" from a podium. The physically robust Steele, a dynamo before an audience, would have been a tough act to follow at conventions and bottling plant openings. Tom preferred to stick with his routine. But he did agree to accept the title of executive vice-president and assume a seat on the board. The ball was now back in Barnet's court. He still needed a president.

There were no Steele's on the horizon, but Tom told Barnet his second choice, Donald Kendall, was acceptable, although Tom might have preferred another executive, Tommy Thompson. Under Kendall, Tom's title of executive vice-president would mean no loss of authority over his realm of the business, or so Tom understood. For Barnet's sake, Tom's was a vital consent, because Kendall was by no means the unanimous choice of the board.

Tom says that Kendall, in fact, probably would have been fired years earlier if Joan Crawford or O'Connell had gotten their way. "Kendall detested Crawford," Tom remembers. He couldn't get along with her in any way because she used to travel a lot for advertising and promotion, and she got all the attention. He was a jealous and conniving man, no doubt about it." Joan had been heard insisting to her husband several times that Kendall be sent packing, only to have Barnet intercede on his behalf with Steele. Joan nicknamed Kendall "Fang," which did not mean he sank his teeth into his work. More than four years after Steele's death, Joan was still battling Kendall from her position on the board. And even O'Connell's patience with Kendall wore out after one 1961 trip, according to Tom: "We were coming back from Africa, O'Connell, myself, Kendall, and Morty Hayes, who was a board member. On the plane, O'Connell says to me, 'Tommy as soon as we get back, we're gonna get rid of him.' Because he could see how this guy was operating everything for himself. I said, 'Let's go for it.' And right after we got back, O'Connell died."

Several board members were skeptical about Kendall's appointment to the presidency, if not openly hostile. It was a classic instance of battling corporate policy cliques, so Pepsi's unofficial arbiter of disputes, Thomas Elmezzi, had to intercede again. "I don't say Kendall wasn't any good," he points out now. "He was very good at some things. Advertising, promotion, publicity—excellent. As a front man, he was great. He had the stature, and he could speak well. I give him credit where credit is due." When Tom gave his O.K., Kendall's path to the presidency was cleared. This meant radical changes were in the offing. Some were positive, because like Tom, Kendall was a go-getter. Others weren't as promising, because unlike Tom, Kendall was prone to sacrifice human considerations on the altar of expediency. As events played out, Othello's vote had helped elect Iago as president of Pepsi-Cola.

⟫•◆•⟪

At this point it's useful to listen to a couple of other voices from Pepsi's past. Peter K. Warren is an 82-year-old former Pepsi executive from Wilton, Connecticut, who retired in 1985 after 35 years. Warren worked for Coca-Cola until 1950, and then joined Pepsi one year after Al Steele made the same jump. But Warren emphasizes that Steele hadn't "brought him along." Their career paths were parallel but not linked; Warren started with Pepsi not in sales, but as a copywriter. In 1957 he moved to the international side, later becoming president of PepsiCo International, newly formed after the merger with Frito-Lay. As fellow globetrotters, Warren and the man he still calls Tommy formed a friendship that continues to this day.

Matter-of-factly and without relish, Warren affirms that enmity existed between disparate constituencies at Pepsi. As a former Coke employee, Warren himself was viewed suspiciously by "Kendall's people." They saw him as a "Steele man," apparently unaware that Steele and Warren had barely known each other at Coke. Such jealousies were no more endemic to Pepsi than anywhere else. Rivalries are found more often in large companies because the management control needed to neutralize discord is diffused. But jealousy creates management imbalances nonetheless. Tom's value as a mediator at Pepsi derived from his friendships with original Loft's Candy Co. people on one side, and Phoenix Securities/Pepsi-Cola interests on the other. But he of course couldn't mollify every Pepsi executive who felt threatened by a transfer-in from Coke.

Warren describes Tom as clinging stubbornly to out-of-fashion notions of reciprocal loyalties—employer for employee, employee for employer, colleague for colleague. "Tommy," says Warren, "couldn't understand it, in fact took it personally, when someone he trusted and liked was compromised without just cause. It bothered him deeply. It went against everything he stood for."

Norman Heller of Stamford, Connecticut, retired from PepsiCo in 1989 after 28 years, having established the company's first International Marketing Research Department early in his career. Later he rose to senior vice-president for the Western Hemisphere (Canada, Mexico, and points south) and to president of PepsiCo Wine & Spirits, which in the 1970s, despite the Cold War, arranged the purchase of Stolichnaya Vodka and made breakthroughs in Romania and

Hungary. He worked closely with Tom through the 1960s, and like so many of Tom's former colleagues, has kept in touch with him. Heller emphasizes Tom's integrity, wisdom, and competence. "He was candid. He wasn't afraid to disagree."

But that's not what Kendall wanted. He assumed the presidency with a mindset similar to newly elected U.S. Presidents, especially when the previous occupant of the White House was from the other party. The existing Cabinet and presidential staff are of course regarded as part and parcel of the preceding administration, but so is much of the bureaucracy. Kendall decided that as incoming president, he was entitled to clean house, almost as if Pepsi's incumbent vice-presidents had been Secretaries of Agriculture and Commerce, and its department heads ambassadors to Turkey and Singapore. Kendall equated employees who had spent entire careers at the company with public servants who enter government at the request of a president and serve for four or eight years, then return home.

In other words, Kendall took a political approach to a situation that Tom viewed from a human resources perspective. To him, these colleagues had given much of their lives to Pepsi, and they were his friends besides. He and Kendall were destined to bang heads. Trouble was brewing at 500 Park Ave.

"He wanted to make so many changes," remembers Tom. "How can you say somebody is no good if you've got them working there 20, 25 years? There must have been some reason you kept them for 25 years, and all of a sudden you don't want them anymore? For what reason? Give me a reason. It was just because he wanted his own man in that position. I think he was trying to be an absolute dictator. He would have liked to fire me the day he became president, but he couldn't, because I had a contract. In 1963 I was given a new contract for five years."

One target of Kendall's was Pepsi's financial vice-president, Lou Nufer, Tom's companion on that plane with the open door in Uruguay. Kendall wanted to put in a man from the international side, Herman Schaefer. "My desk was right outside the boardroom," says Tom, and one day Kendal comes and sits down right across from me and says, 'Tom, we have to fire Nufer.' I say, 'What?' He says, 'I want him out.' I say, "No, no way.' He says, 'What do you mean?' I say, 'No, he stays.'" Tom cited Nufer's longevity and competence, and soon emphasized his disagreement by renewing his friend's contract for five years. Tom could be an independent cuss when questions of personal loyalty were involved.

Kendall eventually got his way, although Pepsi did honor Nufer's new contract. Schaefer was installed, but the new president apparently wanted people to think there had been no challenge to his dictum, because in 1964, when the prospectus was prepared detailing the Pepsi/Frito-Lay merger agreement (finalized in 1965), Herman A. Schaefer was cited as "Pepsi-Cola's financial vice-president since 1963." The last part was untrue; Nufer had been C.F.O. that entire year. The error seems clearly a way for Kendall to save face.

Tom and Kendall would also lock horns over the fate of the Doctors Nachtigall, an uncle and nephew Pepsi had on board to run the company's corporate wellness program. Kendall wanted to bring his own medics in; Tom thought the Nachtigalls had been doing a fine job. In this case, Tom won the battle; the residents stayed in residence, but Tom earned one more demerit in Kendall's black book.

Kendall also wanted to dump the law firm that had represented Pepsi since the *Loft's v. Guth* days and replace it with Nixon, Mudge & Guthrie, the firm where the former vice-president had landed after he lost the election for governor of California in 1962. Nixon was a longtime friend of Kendall's. Pepsi's board still included members from the original firms, some of whom opposed the change. But in this case Tom supported it, and his position prevailed. "As I say, some things you do right, some things you don't. But I don't regret anything I did. If I look at it personally, it was the wrong move. If I look at it for the good of the company at the time, it was right."

⋙◈⋘

In November 1963, Tom flew to Dallas for a Pepsi bottlers' convention. Jeanne traveled with him. It seemed a routine occasion, except that early negotiations for a major corporate acquisition were on the table. At a Friday breakfast meeting in the offices of the First National Bank, Tom sat with bank Chairman Robert H. Stewart III, Donald Kendall, and Pepsi-Cola's newest public relations spokesman, the redoubtable Richard M. Nixon. Two days before, across town, at a Coke national bottlers' convention, Vice-President Lyndon B. Johnson had paid tribute to bottlers everywhere in a speech. L.B.J., for that moment only, put aside his long-standing special relationship with Coca-Cola; it must have required an effort, because by 1963 Coke had established a presence as the Democrats' favorite drink. That sounds silly, but it isn't, because somehow the cola wars had already morphed into an economic adjunct of the two-party system. This was a bizarre phenomenon that Johnson never discouraged and Nixon fairly embraced. Here, two separate bottler conventions were being conducted in the same city in the same week, which brought this odd cola-politics combination into the open.

Mr. Stewart was hosting the Pepsi executives that Friday because his bank had been pegged to provide financial services for Pepsi's tentative merger with Frito-Lay, a pet project of Kendall's that Tom also favored. The breakfast meeting was pleasant. Plans for the future were discussed amiably, but it broke up without much in the way of details because Mr. Nixon had to catch a plane for New York. By 10:30 a.m. he was in the air. The others returned to the convention hotel. Soon thereafter came word from Dealey Plaza, a short distance away, that President Kennedy had been shot while riding in a motorcade. He died minutes later at Parkland Memorial Hospital. Johnson took the oath of office as President on Air Force One, while flying back to Washington.

Pepsi's convention ended abruptly. Jeanne flew home later that day. Tom left Saturday. Both arrived home in time to turn on the TV Sunday morning and watch Jack Ruby murder Lee Harvey Oswald.

⟫—◆—⟪

In 1964, Tom again played an important mediator's role at Pepsi. It might have been a coincidence, but Kendall's rise to the presidency presaged the most serious labor strife anyone at the company had seen since the days when Charles Guth was imprisoned inside his own office in 1935. Now, 13 locals (led by the bottler's union) under an AFL-CIO umbrella went on strike. Without being appointed, Tom assumed responsibility for handling negotiations on the management side. He was the logical choice, given his seat on the board, his title of executive vice-president, and his experience working with bottlers.

Tom was and is no great fan of unions. He had opposed labor's first attempts to organize the Pepsi facilities in Long Island City back in the Depression. "I fought the union at that time. As far as I was concerned, I wasn't gonna have the union. They did organize the bottling plant in the '30s. But they never organized the lab. And to this day I feel the same way. Eventually a certain portion of the lab work was organized, but they wanted to control the whole business, so if they get the labs, they get the bottling plants, and they get the trucks, they have the whole thing locked up. If I went along with them and they organized the lab, today you'd have a lab completely controlled by the union."

By the 1960s, of course, Tom was used to dealing with unions, but if he had been a political animal, he would have realized that this strike put him in a no-win situation. When he suggested to Kendall that Pepsi settle, the boss responded gruffly, "We'll settle when it snows in July." Kendall added, referring to the head of the local who had initiated the job action, "We'll have that guy thrown in jail," without specifying what "that guy" had done to warrant being arrested. Since Tom happened to be dealing with a group that included Hoffa and organized-crime leader Anthony Provenzano, he tactfully avoided passing Kendall's sentiments along, suspecting that his opponents might resent being threatened with imprisonment by a corporate executive in a sharkskin suit. "It was the soft-drink union, part of the Teamsters. Supposedly led by Jimmy Hoffa. Well, he had nothing to do with it. I was in his office, and I know what it's all about. They say he was the big boss, but the fellow I had sitting with me, he was *his* boss, and nobody would ever know it. He was part of the Gambino family. I dealt with them all."

There are indications that the union resented Tom anyway. As the strike dragged on into 1965, Pepsi's lawyer, Peter DeLuca, warned Tom about a phone call DeLuca had received and summarized as, "They're out to get you." Tom didn't know specifically who "they" were (probably not soda bottlers), but he saw fit from then on to ride with a bodyguard at his side. DeLuca was likewise afforded protection.

Meanwhile, as Tom recalls it, "Pepsi management" (suddenly a third-party removed from him) suspected its office phones at 500 Park Ave. were being illegally bugged. Tom believes to this day that some higher-up thought he was conspiring with the "enemy" or wanted others to suspect as much. Whatever the reasons, Pepsi summoned the police. A grand jury was called to investigate, and Tom was called as a material witness. The jury found nothing indictable, and in February 1965, Pepsi finally settled with the strikers on exactly the same terms that were available nine months earlier. "It cost them $25 million in the meantime," Tom insists.

⎯⎯◆◆⎯⎯

Through the strike, Kendall continued to pursue a merger with Frito-Lay. He had made it plain that his growth plans for Pepsi included acquisitions, and he believed Frito-Lay, with its array of salty snacks, offered the perfect partner. But the board was divided. Tom saw it as a no-brainer, a marriage of two companies, each worth close to $300 million and with compatible product lines. The combined weight of the two balance sheets would enable more favorable financing, needed for future growth. (Eventually, Pepsi also acquired Pizza Hut and Taco Bell.) As the deal was structured, a new conglomerate, PepsiCo Inc., would survive, with Frito-Lay boss Herbert Lay as chairman and Donald Kendall as operating head. It sounded logical to Tom. But almost half the Pepsi board, prominently including Joan Crawford Steele, didn't like the idea. They offered various objections, which in Tom's view came down to their not wanting to lose their share of control over Pepsi's business, and/or reduced or forfeited roles. None could offer a solid business rationale for rejecting the proposal, which would have been the only way to change Tom's mind. Kendall was pushing the deal hard, and he knew his foes included the same people who hadn't wanted him to be president.

Again, Tom's recommendation would decide things, and while he'd already come out in favor informally, it wasn't over 'til it was over. In Tom's words: "The board members did not want it, and I had to convince them to do it. Otherwise they still would not have done it, and we would have been in the creek by now. Even Joan Crawford was against me, and we were pals all along. But for the good of the company it was a great thing to do. If you have a $300 million company and another $300 million company, you've got $600 million to go against a competitor. So it would have been wrong for me not to make sure it went through. You can't sit back; you have to go forward. They weren't thinking far enough ahead. All they saw was that Pepsi was successful. Well, Pepsi isn't successful anymore just as Pepsi, the beverage. But Frito-Lay has been very successful. Would I do it again, knowing I would get thrown out of the company? Yes, I would. Because it was the right thing to do."

As events developed, Tom was in New York's University Hospital recovering from the removal of a cyst when the matter came to a vote. Kendall, along with Pepsi C.F.O. Herman Schaefer and Peter Warren, went to the hospital together and strode past the nurses to Tom's bedside. Warren, Tom's longtime friend, asked him how he was feeling. The other two weren't too concerned about that. They simply wanted Tom's reply to a vital question: Would he officially advocate to the board that Peps-Cola merge with Frito-Lay?

Tom wasn't about to ruin their day. Yes, he would make that recommendation. It had been a Kendall deal all the way, but whatever Tom's feelings about the man, he knew the merger marked a positive turning point for Pepsi. He gave his blessing, and that made it a fait accompli. The nurses came back to change Tom's dressings.

With that decision, however, Tom sealed his fate at Pepsi, because the deal gave Kendall control over the board. "The agreement was that if we merged, Frito-Lay would have five members on the board. We had nine on the board before, and now we raised it to 12. He had the Frito-Lay members in his pocket, and with himself, that was six. After a while some of our old board members quit, and he appointed new ones. So he got control, which is what he wanted all along."

After the merger, the friction between Tom and Kendall continued. "As far as I know," says Tom, "I never did anything to harm him. But he had people behind my back trying to sabotage me. You can't operate like that. One of us eventually had to go."

Kendall, Tom believes, was irritated that Tom still exercised considerable